Mariken van Nieumeghen

Medieval Texts and Translations, a subseries of *Studies in German Literature, Linguistics, and Culture,* is edited by Evelyn Sherabon Firchow. It includes important medieval works dealing with the Germanic Middle Ages translasted into the contemporary American idiom. Each tranlation is based on a single manuscript or printed version, which, when feasible, accompanies the translation.

Mariken van Nieumeghen

A Bilingual Edition

Edited, Translated, and with an Introduction by

Therese Decker

Martin W. Walsh

CAMDEN HOUSE

Copyright © 1994 by
CAMDEN HOUSE, INC.

Published by Camden House, Inc.
Drawer 2025
Columbia, SC 29202 USA

Printed on acid-free paper.
Binding materials are chosen for strength and
durability.

All Rights Reserved
Printed in the United States of America
First Edition

ISBN:1-879751-20-8

Library of Congress Cataloging-in-Publication Data

Mariken van Nieumeghen. English & Dutch (Middle Dutch)
   Mariken van Nieumeghen = (Mary of Nijmegan) : a bilingual edition / edited, translated and with an introduction by Therese Decker and Martin W. Walsh.
      p. cm. -- (Studies in German literature, linguistics, and culture)
   Includes bibliographical references.
   ISBN 1-879751-20-8
   I. Decker, Therese, 1940- . II. Walsh, Martin W. III. Title. IV. Title: Mary of Nijmegen. V. Series: Studies in German literature, linguistics, and culture (Unnumbered)
PT5443.M3E5 1993
839.3'122--dc20   93-32518
                                                                     CIP

Acknowledgments

This translation was the basis for a production of the play by the Harlotry Players of the University of Michigan under the direction of Martin W. Walsh for the *Festival of Early Drama* at the University of Toronto, May 24, 1992 and at the annual meeting of the American Association of Netherlandic Studies at Calvin College in Grand Rapids, Michigan on June 13, 1992. Support for this production came from the Consulates General of the Netherlands in the U.S.A. and Canada, as well as from the Residential College and the Department of Theater and Drama of the University of Michigan. Special thanks are due to all Harlotry Players involved, especially to Rebecca Novick (Mariken), Kevin Saari (narrator), John Vincent (Moenen), Suzanne Castello (Mary's aunt), Karyl Newman (costumer), and Jennifer Snoeick (set designer).

In addition we wish to thank Moravian College and in particular Mr. Kevin Snyder for the material support and technical advice needed in the production of this publication, and to Gilbert and Sylvia Stengle of Bethlehem, Pennsylvania, for their invaluable help with the translation, and finally to Mrs. Gisela Ray of Moravian College for her patient help with the proofreading of the original text.

Dedicated to the Memory of

Mathilde T. Decker-Lindvers

(November 24, 1905 - March 1, 1990)

Contents

I   Introduction   1

II   *Mariken van Nieumeghen*
Willem Vorsterman edition, Antwerp (ca.1516/18)   24

Mary of Nijmegen
Translation   25

III   List of Corrections of the Vorsterman Edition   135

IV   Select Bibliography   139

The True and Very Strange Story of Mary of Nijmegen
Who Lived for More than Seven Years with the Devil
and Kept Company with Him.

Introduction

EVER SINCE PRUDENS VAN DUYSE in an article published in the *Kunst-en Letterblad, I* ("Mariken van Nijmegen," 1840) suggested that the "Historie van Mariken van Nimweghen" should be given more scholarly consideration, studies about this remarkable late medieval Middle Dutch play have multiplied enormously. Even a cursory survey of the scholarship quickly reveals that nearly all aspects of this play are still subject to an on-going scholarly debate. Only a few facts have been clearly established:

Edition

The oldest known edition is the Dutch chapbook published by Willem Vorsterman of Antwerp in approximately 1515. (Dirk Coigneau, *Mariken van Nieumeghen*, Nijhoffs Nederlandse Klassieken [The Hague: Nijhoff, 1982], 50). The only copy reposes in the Bayerische Staatsbibliothek in Munich. In 1904 P. Leendertz, Jr. published a facsimile edition of this copy with the Nijhoff publishing house. It is this edition which is reproduced here, identified as version *A* in the *Bibliography*.

Author

He or she remains anonymous, though style and content suggest that a member of a *Rederijker*-chamber, that is, a *rhetorician* or *poet* of one of the many amateur poetry societies so popular during the late Middle Ages in the Lowlands, may have been the author. Though Dirk Coigneau, (*Mariken*, Introduction, 44) determined that the language of the poet is predominantly Brabantian, B. van den Berg, in his article "De noordnederlandse afkomst van Mariken van Nieumeghen" (*De Nieuwe Taalgids* 38 [1945]: 114-15) has also suggested — with little justification — that he may have been a Northerner, specifically a *rhetorician* from Nijmegen. More controversial is J. van Mierlo's suggestion that the poetess Anna Bijns (1493-1575) was responsible for *Mary of Nijmegen* ("Anna Bijns en de volksliteratuur in haar jeugd te Antwerpen," *Verslagen en Mededelingen der Koninklijke Vlaamsche Academie voor Taal- en Letterkunde* [1955]:329-72), a theory supported by L. Debaene (*Mariken van Nieumegen* [Zwolle: W. E. J. Tjeenk Willink, 1958]) and vigorously rejected by L. Roose ("Is Anna Bijns ook de auteur van volksboeken, met name van Floris ende Blancefloor en Mariken van Nieumeghen?" *Jaarboek van "De Fonteine"* [1950]: 42-54) and P. Maximilianus ("Over vorm en auteur van Mariken van Nieumeghen," *Tijdschrift voor Nederlandse Taal- en Letterkunde* 68 [1950]: 161-79).

Little else about this play can be stated with any degree of certainty. The prose-prologue mentions a specific historical event during which the action of *Mary of Nijmegen* takes place. In the year 1465 Count Arnold of Gelderland was imprisoned by his son in the city of Grave; the prose introduction to the suicide of Mary's aunt mentions that he had been set free, an event which took place in February 1471. C. H. A. Kruyskamp, in his *Introduction* to the 5th edition of the play (*Mariken van Nieumeghen*, Klassieke Galerij, 66, 5th, rev. ed. [Amsterdam: De Wereldbibliotheek; Antwerp: De Nederlandsche Boekhandel, 1972], XI-XV) reprints the sequence of events as recorded by Arend van Slichtenhorst in 1654.

These facts, plus internal dates furnished by the poet, have suggested to L. Debaene, in the *Introduction* to his edition of *Mariken van Nieumeghen*, the following reasoning: Mary/Emily lived with the devil for more than seven years, as the title states, and at the time of her conversion her aunt had been dead for three years. Her uncle lived another twenty-four years after her entrance into the Convent of Reformed Sinners in Maastricht, where he visited her faithfully every year. Mary herself lived another two years after the iron rings had been miraculously removed. If this occurred after the death of her uncle then that would have been twenty-six years after her conversion. Thus, Debaene and others argue, the original story must have been written sometime around 1516-18.

This reasoning gives much credence to an author who, it has been determined, is not always reliable. He states the facts correctly about the imprisonment of Duke Arnold by his son; yet he does not seem to have been acquainted with the details of the release of the old Duke. His knowledge of geography was none too sure, since he states in the prose-prologue that Gisbrecht lived a little more than three miles outside of Nijmegen, while Mary/Emily begs Moenen to let her visit her uncle in Venlo which is much further away. It has been argued that the author chose Venlo because it was a city much better known in and around Antwerp. Such an argument would indicate that the author was capable of a certain amount of arbitrariness when it suited his purpose.

W. A. F. Janssen, in his article "Studies over Mariken van Nieumeghen," (*Leuvense Bijdragen: Bijblad*, 56 [1967]: 1-99) subjects these so-called contradictions to careful scrutiny. First, he believes to have proven that, based on stylistic, grammatical and linguistic comparisons, prose and poetry of the play were produced by two different authors; that the prose writer was better informed and on the whole more erudite; and that all internal contradictions were created by the author of the poetry, who was not as well acquainted with the historical details and geography of Gelderland.

Though Janssen's arguments, suggesting two authors, may have some merit, for the sake of convenience only the singular of poet will be used here. And given the kind of drama we are dealing with, it seems just as likely that the poet cared little about the precise logic of internal time indications. Certainly, the number seven is part of the medieval number symbolism, while the twenty-two years of strict penance endured by Mary may have been chosen to impress the audience with the severity of her sins and the suffering required to atone for them. Further, it has been presumed that the action of the play begins with the imprisonment of Duke Arnold, thus in 1465. Yet, the prose-prologue states: "In den tijde dat...," (p. 24) which is translated by us as "In the days when...," (p. 25) which indicates a longer space of time, that is, "during the time when these troubles were taking place." It actually makes more sense within the play to date the start of the play at the time of the release of the old Duke, in 1471. As the prose passage, which introduces the important scene between the girl and her aunt, indicates, Mary arrives at her aunt's house when the latter had already heard about the release of the old Duke; and the aunt, a follower of the young Duke Adolf, is outraged and vents her frustrations on the poor girl who runs crying out of the city to become an easy target for Moenen's seductive powers. The seduction scene is followed by a short prose passage introducing the scene between Gisbrecht and his sister, Mary's aunt: "After Mary, who is now called Emily, had been gone for several days," (p. 55) the uncle begins to worry and decides to go in search of her. At first the aunt denies any knowledge of Mary's whereabouts, but finally admits that "it was eight or ten days ago when she came here." (p. 59) One may wonder why the uncle waited so long to become sufficiently worried to start his search; nevertheless, these two time indications at least do not conflict with one another. The prose passage following the scene between Gisbrecht and his sister introduces the suicide of the aunt and merely repeats and elaborates part of the information already supplied in the prose passage introducing the scene between Mary and her aunt. The release of the older Duke is the only motivation supplied for the aunt's outrageous behavior vis à vis her niece and it seems logical to conclude that Moenen, having returned to Nijmegen with the girl after an approximate seven year sojourn in Antwerp, is simply lying when he tells Emily that her aunt has been dead for about three years. If this were indeed a true statement, it would mean that it took the aunt about four years to enter into a state of extreme outrage and desperation to decide to commit suicide. This makes no sense either from a dramatic or from a historical point of view. One is almost forced to conclude that the author mentions specific dates and historical events in the drama in order to support his claim that he is telling a true story. What we do know with absolute certainty about the dating of the play is, that it must have been written after both historical events had already taken place, namely the imprisonment in 1465 as well as the release of Duke Arnold in 1471. Thus, one may conclude that the drama was written sometime after 1471 but several years before the publication of Vorsterman's chapbook at approximately 1516-1518.

Ever since M. E. Kronenberg published the results of her comparative investigations in the article "Het mirakelspel van Mariken van Nieumeghen en het Engelsche volksboek" (*De Nieuwe Taalgids*, 23 [1929]: 24-43) all scholars seem to agree that Willem Vorsterman's chapbook edition cannot be the original version of the story. The English prose version, *Mary of Nemmegen*, published by Jan Doesborch of Antwerp, also of approximately 1518 (No. 5, *D* in our Bibliography), makes apparent that the translator/adaptor could not have worked with the Vorsterman edition, since some important differences in the two versions make this highly unlikely. Thus, it has been argued, both versions must be based on one or more earlier versions of the story. A great deal of scholarly effort has gone into trying to answer several questions about the nature of this original *Mariken van Nieumeghen*:

1. Was the original tale written in prose which the dramatist recast into dramatic poetry, and are the interpolated prose-introductions of the Vorsterman edition remnants of its original nature? M. E. Kronenberg in particular (ibid., 24) posits that the English prose tale is not a translation of the Vorsterman edition, but rather of an earlier Middle Dutch prose tale which was later reworked into a drama; and the prose fragments of the Vorsterman edition are evidence of its original form. W. A. F. Janssen ("Studies over Mariken van Nieumeghen," *Leuvense Bijdragen: Bijblad*, 56 [1967]: 34) agrees with this interpretation of the facts.

2. Could the original have been written in poetry which contained rhymed narrative passages? A. J. Barnouw ("Mary of Nimmegen," *The Germanic Review*, 6 [1931]: 77-80) in particular is a defender of this theory in that he firmly believes that the prose-introductions are adaptations of what was originally all in rhymes. Barnouw is supported in his views by W. H. Beuken (*Mariken van Nimmegen* 3rd ed. [Zutphen: Thieme, 1972], 23-31) and G. W. Wolthuis (*Diuvelskunsten en Sprookjesgestalten: Studien over Literatuur en Folklore: Mariken van Nieumeghen* [Amsterdam: V. H. C. de Boer Jr., 1952], 61-67).

3. If the prose introductions are later additions, should they be considered part of the drama and, indeed, are they even necessary to an understanding of the play? That is, could they simply be left out as unnecessary interruptions of the flow of the action? P. Leendertz, Jr., in his edition of the play in *Middelnederlandsche dramatische poëzie* (Bibliotheek van middelnederlandsche letterkunde, 2 vols. [Leiden: A. W. Sijthoff, 1907] CXXIV and CCXI) supports this controversial theory by relegating the prose passages to footnotes and by changing the title of the work from "...Een seer wonderlijcke *historie* van Mariken..." to "Een scoon *spel* van Mariken..."

All positions have their ardent defenders who marshal convincing arguments based on detailed philological examinations of the Dutch and English texts of *Mariken van Nieumeghen* and other Middle Dutch plays of the same period. Indeed, so much outstanding work has gone into proving either the priority of a prose or poetic version of the original story that they finally tend to cancel each other out, since cogent reasons for maintaining either of these theories exist. Point three, however — the prose passages are superfluous and can be left out — seems to convince the least. Close examination of the purpose of these passages have led scholars such as Coigneau, who essentially agrees with the positions of Kronenberg and Janssen, to observe that they do furnish vital information to the audience without which parts of the play might become incomprehensible. They also describe events which would be difficult or even impossible to dramatize, such as the journey to Cologne and Rome, and Mary's entry into the convent. From a purely practical point of view, these passages also make it possible for the actors to move from one scene to the next while the audience is occupied with listening to the reciter of the prose.

On the other hand, apart from the aunt's suicide, nothing in the story of *Mariken van Nieumeghen* is at all dependent upon the events surrounding the imprisonment and release of the elder Duke Arnold. In the dramatic text, the aunt does mention her devotion to a "young Duke" and how the release of the "old thief" has enraged her, enraged her to the point of calling up a devil to precipitate her own suicide. The narrative's furnishing of actual names, locales, and an implied chronology hardly helps to make this episode any more plausible from a modern psychological point of view. The aunt's suicide and the lesson drawn from "blind partisan politics" are really side-issues. Drawing just on the information furnished by the *dramatic* text, a contemporary audience, having a historical memory going back at least one generation, would have been able to recognize the events and personalities hinted at by the aunt in her rage. This would be all that was needed. And we certainly do not need a "political" motivation for the aunt's earlier shabby treatment of Mary. It needs to be — and is — *gratuitous* spite, the fairy-tale hate of the old for the young, of the relative for the orphaned child. The seemingly careful contextualization performed by the narrative links, then, is merely embroidery of the plot, not vitally essential information necessary for the play to proceed. Seen from this point of view, the whole question of the chronology of composition of the text, and of Mary's fictional biography — both based exclusively upon the narrative links — seems idle.

It is not our purpose to argue the absolute priority of a dramatic over a narrative original *Mariken van Nieumeghen*. Rather that, if the text as we have it shows sufficient independence as a play-script, then one has the obligation to analyze it as the play, *Mariken van Nieumeghen*. The narrative portions, however, should not, indeed cannot be totally jettisoned. There are places where they serve the function of elaborate "stage directions," where they are, as we shall argue, records or residues of "dumb show" components of the play. But apart from these instances, which largely go to bolster the generic if not the chronological priority of the dramatic text, little use will be made of the narrative linking passages in the staging reconstruction.

Thus, *Mariken van Nieumeghen* can easily be staged in the form in which it has been preserved for us in the Vorsterman edition. Yet, there are no records that it was ever performed in the sixteenth or seventeenth century. Indeed, on April 16, 1621, the bishop of Antwerp put the text on the index of forbidden books, not only for the schools but also "the general public." (Kruyskamp, *Mariken van Nieumeghen*, 5th ed., "Introduction," XXII). The first modern production took place in 1892 in Antwerp as a pantomime performance on two wagons. (W. H. Beuken, *Mariken van Nieumeghen*, Klassiek letterkundig Pantheon 170, 3rd augm. ed. [Zutphen: W. J. Thieme, 1972], 33).

But the episcopal prohibition of the play may in fact not have been the only reason why this very effective drama was not performed before the late 19th century. Other important historical events, directly related to the content of the play, may also have been influential in keeping it out of public view. Thus, in 1484 Pope Innocent issued the bull *summis desiderantes* in which he maintained that all of Germany was filled with devils, witches and sorcerers. Two inquisitors, priests of the Dominican order, Heinrich Krämer [Hendrik Institoris, pseud.] and Jacob Sprenger published the definitive handbook on witchcraft *Malleus maleficarum* in 1487. (W. H. Beuken, *Mariken van Nieumeghen*, Klassiek letterkundig Pantheon 170, 3rd augm. ed. [Zutphen: W. J. Thieme, 1972], 21). According to Wolthuis, in his study *Duivelskunsten en Sprookjesgestalten: Studien over Literatuur en Folklore: Mariken van Nieumeghen* ([Amsterdam: V. H. C. de Boer, Jr., 1952]) and Frans Krap, in *Emmeken: Ik ben 'sduuels amie: neerslag van een onderzoek naar het heksenprofiel van rond 1500 en van het speuren naar onderdelen daarvan in het drama Marieke van Nieumeghen* (Tekst en Tijd, 8 [Nijmegen: Alfa, 1983]), Mary/Emily clearly follows the descriptions of the *Malleus maleficarum*. Thus, Mary calls upon the devil twice, repeats her submission to Moenen and her rejection of God three times, as is prescribed. After some hesitation she agrees to change her name, though insists on keeping the first letter in its diminutive form: Emmeken/Little M. On the other hand, she readily agrees to avoid blessing herself with the sign of the cross. Moenen offers to teach her the "seven liberal arts" while he makes every effort to talk her out of wanting to learn "necromancy", which would have given the girl exceptional powers over her diabolical seducer. Other important signs of her having made a true pact with the devil are Moenen's promise to teach her all the languages of the world and her inability to shed tears until she feels true remorse.

Although Mary herself never practices any witchcraft — only Moenen boasts that he can foretell the future, find hidden treasure, and so forth — yet, Mary is still guilty of having made a pact with the devil. It is therefore astonishing that Mary is not arrested as a confessed witch. Even if it would seem natural that her uncle might be reluctant to hand his niece over to the responsible authorities, one might have expected that at least the "most learned and pious priests" of Nijmegen, to whom she officially confesses herself, would do the expected, namely proceed against her with a witch trial. Neither do the highest ecclesiastic authorities, the bishop of Cologne and the Pope, feel it necessary to accuse the girl of this most heinous crime and draw the appropriate legal consequences. This, too, has led scholars to come to divergent conclusions. Was the play written by a conservative, pro-Dominican poet as a warning against all "dangerous knowledge" including the liberal arts which were coming under the revolutionary influence of early humanism and the rediscovery of classical texts? Or, as others have maintained, is the message of the play that no one, neither priest, bishop nor pope, should pass final judgement on a sinner, but rather leave such decisions in the hands of God? The latter conclusion would imply that the poet envisioned a direct relationship between God and man, an astonishingly proto-protestant concept for this time. It is, therefore, not at all surprising that the play found itself quickly on the index of forbidden books, "ubi necromantia docetur," but also as a dangerous bearer of ambiguous religious and moral messages.

It has been observed that *Mariken van Nieumeghen* partakes of the traditions surrounding the worship of the Holy Virgin as intercessor between God and mankind. For example, Mary maintains contact with her former innocent state by insisting that she be allowed to keep the first letter of her given name, "M". Moenen complains several times that only Uncle Gisbrecht's regular prayers to the Holy Virgin have prevented him from breaking Mary's/Emily's neck long ago. On the road to Cologne Moenen tries to kill the two pilgrims by throwing chunks of wood at them; but not only the power of the Holy Sacrament which Gisbrecht carries with him prevents any harm befalling them, but also God does not permit their deaths because of Mary's/Emily's daily little prayer to His mother, the Holy Virgin. These demonstrations of the power of the Holy Virgin would not seem particularly miraculous to a late medieval audience; in fact, given the popularity of the special devotion to the Holy Virgin during this period, it would consider them as a routine part of daily religious practice. But the miracle of Mary's conversion through the intercession of the Holy Virgin, after having spent more than seven years in the company of the devil, living a seductively sumptuous life, would have made a great impression. This is why *Mariken van Nieumeghen* has generally been classified with the traditional miracle plays as they had been popularized in Paris. Yet, already in 1924, Adriaan J. Barnouw, in his introduction to Harry Morgan Ayres' English translation of *Mariken van Nieumeghen* (*Mariken van Nimmegen: A Marvelous History of Mary of Nimmegen, Who for More than Seven Years Lived and Had Ado with the Devil* [The Hague: M. Nijhoff, 1924], 1) indicates that this may be a miracle play of a special kind.

In fact, as he recalls the story of the traditional miracle legend of *Beatrijs*, in which the Holy Virgin had personally replaced the fallen girl and taken up her duties in the convent, he calls the story of *Mariken van Nieumeghen* a "grotesque caricature" of this earlier tale. And L. Debaene, in the introduction to his edition of 1958, (*Mariken van Nieumegen*. Klassieken uit de Nederlandse Letterkunde [Zwolle: W. E. J. Tjeenk Willink, 1958], 14, note 2) observes, "Not because of the words of the priest, her uncle, but rather because of the play did Mary arrive at self-reflection." But then he qualifies this observation: "Nevertheless, we do not dare assert that it was the conscious intention of the author to contrast the power of the literary work with the spiritual admonition of priests." Nevertheless, Mary is not saved by the direct intercession of the Holy Virgin, but rather by watching a play in which an actor — perhaps even an actress — enacts the role of the Holy Virgin. Thus, Mary is led to reconsider her sinful life by a work of art, indeed, poetry or "rethorijcke," the oldest among all the arts, the one which is, according to Mary/Emily herself, "a gift of the Holy Spirit." (p. 75) The enactment of the play-within-the-play *Maskeroon* must be interpreted as an especially effective demonstration of the power of poetry. When Mary/Emily begs Moenen to let her watch the play, she claims that her uncle had told her that it "is better than some sermons." (p. 93) This is high — and unusual praise — from such a devout and seemingly conventional priest. *Maskeroon* is staged on a wagon. Though it is true that these pageant wagons could be quite large and equipped with rather sophisticated stage machinery, such as dumbwaiter devices to link Heaven and Hell, simple staging would point up the dramatic effectiveness of the dialogue composed for the three characters, Maskeroon, the devil's advocate, God and the Virgin Mary. It seems that the play was intended to reach beyond the usual pastoral admonitions and warnings and aspire to true dramatic poetry so that not only Mary's/Emily's conversion would seem believable and truly miraculous to the other characters on stage, that is, Moenen and Gisbrecht, but also convince the real audience that the whole play is a persuasive, dramatic example of how one may escape the consequences of even the most sinful kind of life.

The Power of Language

Since the play-within-the-play has such a dramatic impact on the action of the play, it is perhaps not too daring to claim that this seemingly simple, straight-forward little drama about *Mariken van Nieumeghen* carries within itself a sophisticated theory of the role of language and in particular poetry, as one might rename "rhetoric" today. In a sense, the whole play seems to comment on the power of words, their use and abuse, their positive and negative impact on the lives of people. Limited space will not permit a complete investigation of this question, yet it seems appropriate to suggest at least a beginning, to initiate a discussion about the anonymous poet's notions about language and words.

The play begins simply enough. Uncle Gisbrecht gives Mary detailed instructions about what she should buy in Nijmegen, how she is to pay careful attention so as not to be cheated and that she should stay in town if it should get too late to return during daylight hours. Mary is an obedient young girl who seems only concerned with fulfilling her uncle's instructions to the letter. When it has gotten too late to return home, she purposely chooses to greet her aunt politely with a Christian greeting: "Aunt, may Christ ease all your suffering and protect all your loved ones from harm," (p. 31). These seemingly simple lines are really quite ironic in that they state the exact opposite of what is already and will soon become reality. Christ had not protected the aunt from her greatest sorrow, namely the release from prison of the old Duke. Nor does the aunt seem to have anyone she loves, certainly not Mary or her uncle.

More importantly, Mary's charitable good wishes for her aunt have no effect on the aunt, who has become "crazy or more like a raging she-devil than a Christian." (p. 29) In this state of mind the aunt is no longer capable of hearing the Christian message of good-will and reacts as the evil person she has become. Her unwarranted attack on Mary's character and reputation — in the foulest language possible — identifies her as a spiritual companion of the devil, since Moenen is the only other person to employ such language in his monologues and asides. Thus, the aunt is already beyond redemption, unable to come to her senses, to reconsider, to reflect on the state of her soul. Mary, up to this point still the innocent young girl, takes the filthy accusations of her aunt to heart and, in a kind of word-magic, becomes what her aunt has mendaciously called her, a whore, indeed, the whore of the devil, thus demonstrating the power of evil words over even their most innocent victims.

Moenen is also aware of how important language and its usage is when he states that in order to successfully seduce a young woman one must speak politely to her. Even if this observation might be called mundane, his refusal to teach Mary/Emily necromancy nevertheless underscores once again Moenen's awareness of the power of language. For necromancy is nothing less than the ability to control evil spirits — devils — by employing words and phrases in precise, prescribed order. Moenen is determined to control Mary/Emily with his sweet talk, but he will not hand her a tool with which she might gain control over him. Uncle Gisbrecht, on the other hand, successfully employs approved magic formulas of exorcism in order to control and to defeat Moenen. In this manner, dangerous words and phrases are employed for a good cause.

Naturally, Mary's/Emily's hymn to rhetoric, i.e., poetry, is the most precise statement of what the poet thought about the nature of this art. It should not surprise us to note that it is placed almost precisely at the center of the play. In it Mary/Emily bemoans the fact that untalented flatterers are honored everywhere while true poets go hungry. But true poetic art brings happiness and glory to a country where it is appreciated and rewarded. And if a country benefits so greatly by cultivating and supporting true art then it will certainly also have a positive influence on all those who cultivate and love the true art of poetry.

As we know, Moenen promises Mary/Emily to teach her the seven liberal arts. She claims to know logic "inside out" and offers to count the drops of wine in a tankard by employing the rules of geometry. But the only art she actually demonstrates is poetry. And it is poetry, dramatic poetry in this case, which brings about such a stunning change in her life.

The play *Maskeroon* itself is, in spite of its apparent simplicity, quite compelling. At first Maskeroon, the devil's advocate, merely complains that God is more compassionate and merciful toward mankind than toward the poor spirits of hell. After all, the devils sinned only once in one short rebellious thought against God while mankind sins daily in unspeakable ways. Maskeroon forgets to mention that the rebellious devils never confessed — a verbal act — their sin of overweening pride nor suffered contrition. God clearly states that confession and true contrition will earn His forgiveness, without bothering to mention that the fallen angels had had the same moral choice. Then Maskeroon proceeds to enumerate the horrible sins man commits for which he deserves to be punished in the harshest manner. Listening to this recital of iniquity, God becomes angrier and angrier, until He finally agrees with Maskeroon, and decides to inflict His "powerful sword of justice" (p. 97) upon mankind. This is the first dramatic climax: the devil Maskeroon has won his case and God, in His justified anger, is ready to withhold the benefits of His sacrifice from mankind. Only the intervention of the Mother of God, her moving plea on behalf of sinful mankind, turns God's justified wrath into mercy. As had been promised, true repentance will lead to salvation. And thus the second, and final climax as well as the final resolution has been achieved.

This short play, only one-hundred-thirteen verses long, is remarkably effective. It not only makes Mary's/Emily's conversion believable, it also seems to have inveigled some very astute scholars into believing that the girl is saved by the direct intervention of the Holy Virgin, when in reality this remarkable feat is accomplished by actors reciting poetic lines of dialogue on a relatively primitive stage. In *Mariken van Nieumeghen*, this rather strange miracle play, it is not the Mother of God who has once again successfully intervened on behalf of a sinner, but rather the "miracle" of true poetry.

Indeed, when Mary/Emily is carried by Moenen into the air and he throws her to the ground, the girl is not saved from certain death by divine intervention, but rather by luck. As Uncle Gisbrecht, who had been watching the same play, remarks rather prosaically: "She's really lucky if she didn't break her neck!" (p. 107)

Mary's/Emily's further adventures have more to do with her somewhat controversial status as repentant sinner who seeks forgiveness with the proper ecclesiastic authorities. However, her last injunction to the audience is more than a little puzzling and mystifying. In the Middle Dutch original Mary/Emily exhorts the audience:

O mensche vol ghebreken en[de] vol sonden
Hier aen moechdi nemen exempele
En[de] ter eeren deser weerdicheit sonder gronde[n]
Den almoghende god eewighen lof vermonden
Naer v arm macht seer sempele
Weldaet dient wel ghedaen in gods tempele. (p. 130)

We translated this:

Oh sinful, weak mankind! You can learn a lesson from all this and sing the praises of the boundless grace of Almighty God, each as best you can, according to your simple talents. Good works deserve to be performed well in the House of the Lord. (p. 131)

Here the poet clearly establishes a connection between "singing" the praises of God and the talent that is required to do so, even if such abilities are merely artless. But it is the last line which is the most enigmatic. "Good works" may mean nothing more controversial than the good work of penance as endured by Mary/Emily for over twenty years. But this line must have some logical connection with the preceding five lines. Thus, a more daring reading of this line, connecting it with the previous injunction to sing the praise of the Lord, would be:

Good works [of poetry] deserve to be well performed in the House of the Lord,

an interpretation which also seems to have occurred to Harry Morgan Ayres (*A Marvelous History of Mariken van Nimmegen* [The Hague: M. Nijhoff, 1924], 77) which he renders in the following manner:

Praise ye the Lord in His temple for the Lord His sake.

Clearly, the poet of *Mariken van Nieumeghen* seems to have had some very clear ideas about the role of language and poetry. His complex rhyme schemes of the "rondelen" in the "referein" of the scene in the inn, as well as in the several monologues are impressive artistic accomplishments. It seems to have mattered to him a great deal that a knowledgeable audience or reader of his work would understand that he counted himself among the talented poets who used his magical talent with words not only in praise of the Lord but also for the greater glory of poetry.

That he is successful in this endeavor is attested by the fact that the play does not readily fit into any genre one might assign to it. Is it a traditional miracle play about the role of the Holy Virgin as *mediatrix* between God and mankind? Not quite, as we have seen. After all, the only true miracle occurs at the end of the play when God Himself sends an angel to earth to remove the three rings from Mary's/Emily's arms and neck as a sign of His forgiveness. Although probably written by a member of a *Rederijker*-chamber, it is not a morality play in the same sense as *Elkerlijk/Everyman*. The highest Christian authority on earth, the Pope, refuses on the one hand to persecute the girl as a witch, which his office would have obliged him to do; on the other hand he also refuses to grant her absolution by referring the matter directly to God. Nor can one truly claim that the play is a plea for art for art's sake, though the poet seems to have had very definite ideas about the role and power of language and poetry. Rather, the last words which he puts into the mouth of Mary/Emily seem to imply, "true art in the service of God."

As is the case with all masterpieces, the many facets of *Mariken van Nieumeghen* have made it endlessly fascinating to scholars and to lay audiences/readers alike. It has already generated an immense body of scholarship and no doubt will inspire further studies in times to come.

Stage Directions and Performance Reconstruction

To turn now to those features of the text itself which betray its fundamentally dramatic nature, we can mention the following:

a) Use of asides and soliloquies consistent with dramatic writing and dramatic conception.

b) A spatial conception that supplies its own indications of movement.

c) A reliance on elements of spectacle containing clues as to their technical realization.

d) The impressive metatheatricality of the *Maskeroon* play.

There are four distinct *asides* in Moenen's initial interview with Mary — "By Lucifer, this is of great advantage to me!" (p. 43) "Ha, ha, I've talked her out of that!" (p. 49) "If I can't get her to change that name,..." (p. 51) and, significantly, the final line of the scene, "And in the end, I hope, your soul will be lost." (p. 55) Asides, out of earshot of the character(s) in the scene and strictly for the benefit of the audience, are not at all characteristic of the narrative mode, but are quintessential in the dramatic. Their skillful handling in this key scene bespeaks the work of a *playwright* first and foremost. There is even an example of the rather sophisticated technique of an aside *almost* overheard:

Moenen

The prayers of that baldheaded troublemaker have frustrated me often enough whenever I wanted to crush every bone in her body. I would have broken her neck long ago; but his prayers to the Virgin Mary let her escape from me over and over again. I simply never had the right opportunity to carry out my plans as I wanted.

Emily

What did you say, Moenen?

Moenen

Nothing, Emily darling! I give you permission to see your friends after all... (p. 87)

This deliberate breakdown of the technique, and the perceptual double-focus it requires, occurs precisely at the point where it does the most dramatic good: at the point where Moenen is beginning to lose his grip on Emily/Mary.

Soliloquies are less an indication of dramatic conception and writing since they are perfectly at home in the narrative mode as well. Still, the *Mary*-soliloquies are dramatically consistent. Soliloquies in the pure technical sense, the inner state expressed *as if* alone and unobserved, are reserved only for the family — the uncle, Mary, the aunt preceding her suicide, and only for states of intense spiritual distress. Moenen's longer solo speeches are still a species of aside. They require an audience as continuing witness to Moenen's double-game. We may take it as an operating rule in this dramatic universe, therefore, that asides are reserved only for the wily devil and soliloquies only for the suffering human protagonists.

Even more important than this dramatic shaping of the *ensemble* are the many space/time indications in the dramatic portions of the text. Spatially, it calls for a multiple set or "mansion" staging, either in a serial or circular arrangement, common to much of medieval drama. In just the opening passages we need the rectory, the market at Nijmegen some three miles away, the aunt's house in Nijmegen, and a "large thorn bush" some distance out of town. The scale of *Mariken van Nieumeghen's* many locales would tend to favor, then, an outdoor marketplace setting, but there is nothing that absolutely rules out an indoor production, given a spacious enough environment.

What is deeply ingrained in the dramatic text is a sense of onward movement, both physical and spiritual, through a fictive space of Lowland towns and countryside, and through a kind of negative pilgrimage, from error into sin into indifference, to find salvation in the end. These two kinds of journeying are beautifully counterbalanced in a full dramatic presentation. As Mary departs from her uncle's house at the beginning of the play, leaving a piece of stage architecture to enter empty but by no means neutral "travelling space" on the way to the next set, we notice an interesting simultaneity of effect. The uncle, alone now, has a sudden and intense premonition for her safety. Yet he also seems to have Mary still half in view. He in fact signals the audience's own perceptual shift from the one locale to the other, loading it with darkest overtones:

> Lord God, why is my heart so heavy? Is it because the country around here is in such turmoil? Or is it because *my niece there is leaving me?* Well! Why do I suddenly feel so sad? This is very strange! Just as *that girl there left me*, a strange feeling came over me. (p. 29, italics ours)

The speech has considerably more impact if we, the audience, perceive Mary journeying with her shopping basket, rather than have her out of sight "backstage," as would be the case on a proscenium arch stage.

The *length* of Mary's journey to Nijmegen would therefore have to be significant, arguing again for the spaciousness of a full marketplace staging environment. The actual market at Nijmegen, or any other town, could very well have been the "market at Nijmegen" called for in the play, metatheatrical playing with the signification of a site being nothing new to medieval drama. Some theatrically determined booths would be needed, however, to establish a "market" within the market. A representation of the city gate or gates, with perhaps a sign would be all that would be required to establish Nijmegen. We already know from the dramatic text all that Mary is to procure at the market, and so the narrative link is actually redundant here, especially if we postulate a dumb show of market shopping at this point. We will have an on-stage crowd/audience for *Maskeroon* later on, and there is no reason why these extras would not be available now to serve as market people and Mary's fellow customers.

The aunt's house is also within the "city" as established. Here again we have precise indications as to the movement from one playing locale to another. Mary states, "My aunt lives close by. I'll go and ask her if she will give me a bed. ... *I see my aunt standing in front of her door.* ...I'll go and greet her politely." (p. 31, italics ours) Precipitous flight from this "house" into the empty space outside the "city" ends at the symbolically threatening "large, thick thorn-bush" (p. 37) (the narrative's description, but Mary herself refers to "these branches ... under this hedge") (p. 37), where the fatal partnership with Moenen will be formed, ending what amounts to Act I.

The next unit of action recapitulates the movement from the uncle's house to Nijmegen, to the aunt's house, but without our heroine in evidence. The time indications in the text - "eight or ten days ago" (p. 59) - are therefore not as telling as the visual impact of Gisbrecht moving alone through the sequence of locales in his anxiety for Mary's safety. In this fluid form of staging, even minimal movement through space will always predicate large lapses of time. The very fact that Mary is "off" for the whole of this movement (Act II, as it were), presupposes that she is "far away," both spatially and temporally. It would seem that Gisbrecht's soliloquy after the unpleasant interview with his sister is delivered somewhere on the homeward journey. "Act II" ends, then, back in the aunt's house, beyond which the forces of good cannot go.

Admittedly, the aunt's suicide is one of the more difficult incidents of the play to rationalize, given only what we have in the text. Perhaps something "political" is missing from the dramatic portion, or perhaps something has shifted position. How the aunt gets her "news" of the "old thief's" release could perhaps be conveyed by the old device of a letter, but this still would not solve the larger problem. Why bring in this "political" rage at all when, in its current position, the scene could just as well fuel itself from the hatred the aunt bears for her brother and all he stands for? The act of suicide itself, however, is perfectly coherent and highly dramatic. The aunt's raging attracts the attention of a devil. There is some indication of sexual play — "Who's this? To tell the truth, one could have some fun with such a young fellow" (p. 65) — is perfectly in tune with the aunt's dirty mind. And phallic symbolism quickly materializes into a dagger, in the common medieval iconography of suicide, directly offered to the victim by the tempting devil. The aunt "self-destructs," and this bizarre manifestation of the irrational and demonic, this devil-haunted house serves as physical barrier past which Mary cannot get "home."

The third unit of action brings Mary and Moenen on again, abroad in the wide world, approaching Antwerp by way of 's-Hertogenbosch. There has been plenty of time off-stage to transform Mary, the country girl, into a patrician lady and thus enhance the passage of time. "Antwerp" calls for yet another "mansion," the Tavern of the Golden Tree, spacious enough to have two sets of tables and chairs and to serve as the "theater" for Mary's performance of her Praise of Poetry. The narrative link at this point could be interpreted as embodying a stage-direction — a crowd gathers around Mary, and Moenen takes the opportunity to create a riot in which someone is knifed to death — though as usual the narrative carries events beyond what is actually needed for the play — the murderer is subsequently beheaded. The performance of the poem would seem to have no dramatic resolution unless something very much like this transpired immediately after it. Moenen would not need any words, of course, to set a gaping, male, on-stage audience at loggerheads with each other. Conventional slapstick would be enough. The very next moment calls for Moenen, evidently alone on stage, exalting over his powers of disruption. Like Hamlet crowing over the effect of his "Mouse Trap," this speech is best imagined as precipitated out of a scene of great bustle, noise and confusion. The speech, moreover, serves the same function as the narrative's report of the many killings and other crimes precipitated by the couple over time. It gives temporal weight to the sojourn at the Golden Tree, that gilded transformation of the original forlorn thorn-bush.

Mary's agonizing soliloquy then follows, but pangs of conscience are distracted by more low-life: "Hold on! Those two people I see over there! I invited them yesterday for drinks and dinner. Together with them I'll raise my voice in song!" (p. 81) The narrative link says that through this same songfest Moenen caused another death, again an easily managed bit of dumb show, if competition for Mary's attention is presumed. Moenen returns cackling with glee after this second violent clearing of the stage, regaling the audience with more of his mischief. As in Mary's soliloquy, the time signature "yesterday," together with several anecdotes, helps give the impression of the passage of many days. Indeed, the playwright telescopes quite skillfully time and space here. Rather than set himself a cumbersome series of similar events in other "mansion" locales, he uses these two Moenen speeches around a Mary soliloquy and possible further acts of mayhem, to stand for the whole six or seven years of riot and loose living.

When the dramatic text next resumes in what effectively is the fourth unit of dramatic action, we are in the middle of an argument over whether Mary should visit home. Here the dialogue seems to be more dependent on the narrative heading than is usually the case, but the scene might have been conceived as occurring *in medias res,* a devise common enough in later Renaissance drama. The *content* of their argument is certainly recapitulated in the dialogue and poses no problem.

This passage puts the couple on a trajectory back to Nijmegen and the spectacular events of Holy Procession Day. We shall reserve discussion of the interlocking spectacles, the morality play and the portent of Mary's levitation, to pass on to the fifth unit of dramatic action, Mary's penance. Here the narrative would seem to predominate, giving us far too many details in the stages of Mary's purgation and deliverance. Yet even here, if we allow the use of dumb show and processional, a clear and satisfying dramatic line is established according to the principles of staging already indicated.

Immediately after her fall, Mary is led by her uncle "under this roof." (p. 117) She is lodged in a safe house in Nijmegen at long last. It is from this base of operations that Gisbrecht launches the eucharistic procession mentioned in the narrative: "[He] prepared himself as if he were about to celebrate mass by picking up the revered and blessed Holy Sacrament. Protected in this manner he started with his niece Emily on their journey to Cologne." (p. 119) They are harassed by Moenen on the way (too good a character not to bring on one last time), but the power of the Eucharist in procession shields them from all harm. Mary's rejection by the Archbishop of Cologne could be managed in a dumb show, and the procession would then wend its way further on to Rome. Both "Cologne" and "Rome" could easily be the cities of "Antwerp" and "Nijmegen" recycled and refurbished, perhaps with church units within them activated for the first time. Mary receives her penance from the Pope in the shape of heavy iron rings around her neck and arms. Her painfully slow progress *back* along the processional route, as penitent under our gaze, serves as a dramatic shorthand for the "twenty-four years" of her trial. We then move directly on to the House of Repentant Sinners in Maastricht (Gisbrecht's "mansion" recycled?) and her final deliverance. The seemingly complicated series of events which make up Mary's final "Act," then, would not be unmanageable in strictly dramatic terms, if telescoped and compressed along the lines indicated. The combined solemnities of a eucharistic procession, a papal court, a penitential display, and of an angelic, dream-like visitation gives rhythmic weight and counterpoise to the wild, whirling events of "Act IV" and amply conveys in terms of stage-time the protracted penance of Mary.

The wild events just referred to, it might be argued, are just the aspects that would baffle full dramatic realization. They just cannot be done. Up to the levitation and casting down of Mary, the play has proceeded without reliance upon spectacular effects — except, perhaps, for some fire and brimstone to underscore the aunt's suicide. The idea of Moenen raising Mary up in the air and casting her down would seem, then, to be a shock beyond anything we, as audience, are prepared to accept. But this may be just the point. The *spectacle* of Mary suspended in the air and crashing down to earth is Moenen's answer to the spectacle of *Maskeroon*. The latter is a theatrical illusion to be experienced as such within our theatrical fiction. The former is a theatrical illusion that we are meant to accept as a reality within the same fiction. The fake illusion, the play, produces a genuine effect, Mary's repentance. The real illusion, the flight and fall, fails to produce its effect, the horrible death of Mary. The miracle of repentance and the miracle of physical preservation are seen to balance each other.

But is Moenen's theatrical illusion at all feasible? Medieval drama, as we are coming more and more to realize, was capable of some very sophisticated technical effects. To cite but one example from a play we know was performed, in the Croxton *Play of the Sacrament* we find this stage direction: *Here the ovyn must rive asunder and blede owt at the cranys, and an image appere owt with woundys bleeding.* (David Bevington, ed., *Medieval Drama*

[Boston:Houghton Mifflin, 1975], 754-88). The "image" is an actual actor in the role of the crucified Christ who then proceeds to speak. If this oven-effect could be achieved to some degree of satisfaction, then the staging of the Mary-levitation is not as far-fetched as it might appear.

The dramatic text itself affords some clues. Back in the tavern scene Moenen had promised the audience, "I'll perform even more outstanding marvels for you, if there's no interference from God." (p. 83) At the end of *Maskeroon* he makes good on this promise. There is ample indication in the text at this point that Moenen is *dragging* the now repentant Mary off and away from the play-site. He commands her: "Get up, by all the devils," (p. 105) and "Come along, come along!" (p. 107) It is only when he has fully mastered her physically that he makes his intentions known — "I'll carry her up to the dark clouds." (p. 105) There is a crowd of play-goers still on stage who could quite easily form a screen for the substitution of a mannequin at this point. Moenen could achieve sufficient elevation quickly by means of a pulley device anchored to a building, from which height he could cast down the limp mannequin in his arms. The narrative text here seems to point to the fundamental principle of all such theatrical illusions — misdirection. The reaction of the crowd is as big as the illusion itself — "Her uncle and all the people saw this, and they were all greatly astonished, since they did not know what it meant" "This frightened the people very much." (p. 107) There is, moreover, a precise indication in the text that the crowd is serving as a screen for the illusion, in this case for the substitution of the Mary actor/actress for the mannequin. A bystander says to Gisbrecht:

> I want to get a look and see if I know her. But *there's such a crush of people, pushing in such confusion, you can't get there.* Follow me, sir, I'll make room for us! (p. 109, italics ours)

A minor actor facilitates access to the supposedly mangled body. While the actual mechanism of the illusion remains a matter of speculation, evidence such as this sufficiently proves that a practical working out of the illusion is at least feasible.

We would further suggest that Moenen also undergoes a transformation in the course of this action. He may very well remain hovering over the recognition scene at some height, ready to interject his obscenities and demands for Mary's soul. He must now be seen for what he truly is. In the process of misdirection and substitution the Moenen-actor could conveniently don a hideous devil mask. Returning him to the physical level of the crowd in the guise of a mere human being would seem to be inadequate after what has transpired. Moenen's language is far more violent and obscene now. In fact, woodcuts E and F of the Vorsterman edition support such a change in Moenen. Gisbrecht, moreover, begins a formal exorcism which, we might speculate further, actually causes Moenen's mask to fume — "Sparks of hellfire are blowing out of my ears and jaws" (p. 117) — an effect within the celebrated powers of medieval pyrotechnics. Moenen's subsequent appearance in the eucharistic procession, where he vainly hurls uprooted trees at the pair, would then be another occasion for demonic sound and fury now rendered wordless and impotent.

We have already had occasion to mention the crucial importance of the Morality Play of *Maskeroon*. Indeed, it lays claim to being the earliest complete example of the play-within-the-play device in European drama. Its sure handling argues for a dramatic technique of no small sophistication. One cannot imagine this achievement without a vital theatrical context, a thinking in essentially theatrical terms. At its most effective, the play-within-the-play serves as a kind of radio-crystal, transmitting and transmuting various themes of the play at large. The classic example is Shakespeare's *Pyramus and Thisbe*, the Act V entertainment within *A Midsummer Night's Dream*. In the relief of the happy ending, it "replays," now in a burlesque mode and at high speed, the pains of lovers sundered and the terrors of the night. *Maskeroon* had a comparable effect upon the *Mariken/ Mary* play, some hundred years earlier.

Maskeroon, "the devil's lawyer," obviously parallels the learned Moenen in the play proper. Both are descendants of the satanic advocate of the *Book of Job*. Both only act, ultimately, under the sanction of the Deity. In purely physical terms, the "mask" of Maskeroon can even be made to echo Moenen's eye-patch. Maskeroon's examples of human evil, interestingly, are all interfamilial and "unnatural" — as is the aunt's initiating act of hatred — "... a child raped its own mother, or kicked and beat its own father, or one brother accused the other..." (p. 95) In the God-figure's reference to His own shameful and infamous death on the cross we may get a fleeting reminder of Mary "despised and rejected." But Maskeroon's further arguments bring the later fallen Mary/Emily into immediate focus — "...those who obstinately cling to despicable wickedness..." (p. 95). God, raising His sword in righteous anger recalls, inversely, the furious aunt and her dagger.

Naturally, Mary is reading her own story into the courtroom of Heaven and responds accordingly. This is the way a standard Morality Play was meant to work on a hard-hearted audience. But the metatheatricality goes further. The Virgin Mary (the only positive female image in the play), begs that first "signs and portents" be sent to warn mankind. Her Son finds this a waste of effort. "So often in the past I produced signs which should have alarmed them: plagues, wars, famine." (p. 99). And yet the play *Maskeroon* itself is a "sign", and Mary for one is heeding it, whatever else the on-stage crowd is doing about it. The play-within-the-play seems to be warning us, the actual audience, not to treat the events of this sensational plot as mere entertainment — no doubt a constant danger for medieval drama. The Morality Play's teaching, it seems, has to present itself doubled over, turned inside out, so as to prevent its being blunted or easily dismissed. Mary's experience of *Maskeroon* and our empathy with her, then, helps us to experience the subsequent "portent" of Mary as sinner hurled from the sky. The play thus protects its own amazing *coup de théâtre* from mere sensationalism, and integrates it superbly into the action as a whole. The "recognition scene" between uncle and niece has the potential for truly moving pathos, and the technically less demanding miracle of release from the penitential rings becomes paradoxically much more significant. Both are beneficiaries of the play-within-the-play and its epilogue, the diabolical "illusion." The play's conclusion owes much of its controlled effect of joy within solemnity to its bold, even outrageous metatheatricality. Such impressive self-reflexivity bespeaks, again, a mastery of the phenomenology of *theater* beyond the powers of a simple narrative.

About this Edition

The Middle Dutch Text

As mentioned before, the chapbook published by Willem Vorsterman at about 1516/18 forms the basis of this translation. It has been reproduced here as faithfully as possible. All printing errors have been kept in the text with corrections supplied on a separate *List of Corrections*. The end of a line in the prose sections has been indicated in the following manner: if a line ended with a full word a space before and after the slash indicates this; if a line separates a word no spaces were added. Though some editors have felt it necessary to add some lines to the text by comparing the Vorsterman edition to later reprints, no such "corrections" were attempted here. However, all abbreviations have been resolved. The spelling has not been adjusted to modern usage as it is felt that readers will quickly adjust to reading *u* for *v* and vice versa; also note that *i,j* and *y* are employed interchangeably. The decorative paragraph sign in the Vorsterman edition is represented in our transcription and translation by ¶. We have indicated within the text where the original placed the woodcuts; however, we have chosen to incorporate them within the English translation at slightly less than one quarter their original size. The titles in braces are our own additions.

The Vorsterman edition is made up six gatherings of 6, 4, 6, 6, 4, 6 sheets respectively with lettered sheet counters Aiij, Bi, Biij, Ci, Ciij, Di, Diij, Ei, Fi, Fiij. We have supplied the missing sheet counters in braces to the left of text in order to aid the reader in orienting himself within the Middle Dutch text.

The English Translation

This translation supersedes the two previous English renderings. Harry Morgan Ayres's poetic translation of 1924, while still charming in its antiquated style, has nevertheless become almost unreadable — not to say unperformable — for a modern audience; E. Colledge's prose translation suffers from a serious lack of scholarly supporting material. He mentions neither the edition/s he consulted nor the copious scholarly studies devoted to *Mariken van Nieumeghen*. In our edition, no line by line translation was attempted since such a practice would have done violence to English grammar and syntax. Rather, we tried to render the sense of the original as faithfully as possible in modern American prose. Only Mary's/Emily's hymn to poetry has been reproduced in the poetic style of a *rederijker*-poet to set it off from the prose-dialogue. However, a simpler prose translation of the hymn may be consulted at the end of the *List of Corrections*.

The reader will note that the Dutch town *Nijmegen* is spelled in various ways within the Middle Dutch text (nieumeghen, nimmeghen, nyeumeghen), and that scholars of the play also seem at variance about which spelling to choose. We have decided to employ the spelling of the title page of the Vorsterman edition, *Nieumeghen*, in our discussion; the late Middle English prose version of the play published by Jan van Doesborch is referred to as *Mary of Nimmegen*. In our translation of the text we chose to employ the nomenclature of geographical terms of the *Atlas of the World*, 5th edition, 1981, of the National Geographic Society.

Bibliography

The research about *Mariken van Nieumeghen* is vast and we therefore offer merely a selection of the most important works. For material before 1941 consult W. van Eeghem; for 1942 to 1951, A. L. Verhofstede and for the scholarship since 1952, Dirk Coigneau's excellent edition of the play published in 1982.

True and Very Strange Story of Mary of Nijmegen
Who Lived for More than Seven Years with the Devil
and Kept Company with Him.

{A1r}

die waerachtige en[de] / Een seer wonderlijcke historie van Marike[n] van / nieumeghen die meer dan seuen iaren / mette[n] duuel woe[n]de en[de] verkeerde

{Woodcut A}

{A1v}
{A2r}
                  Die prologhe

N[1] den tijde dat hertoghe .Are[n]t van gheldre te[n] / graue gheuanghe[n] wert gheset van sijne[n] sone / hertoghe Olof ende sijne[n] mede pleghers so woen/de op dri milen na Nieumeghe[n] een deuoet priester / gheheeten heer ghijsbrecht en[de] met hem woe[n]de ee[n] / schoon ionghe maecht gheheete[n] .Mariken zijnder / suster dochter wiens moeder doot was. Dese voer/screuen maecht regeerde haers ooms huys he[m] zij[n] / gherief wel eerlijck ende neerstelijck doende

¶ Hoe heer ghijsbrecht . Mariken zijnder nichten / tot Nimmeghen ghesonden heeft

{Woodcut A repeated}

{A2v}

HEt ghebuerde dat des heer Ghijsbrecht mari/ken zijnder nichten seynde[n] wilde in die stadt / va[n] Nieumeghen om daer te coopene tghene dat si / behoefden tot haer seggende aldus

    Mariken

                  {Mariken}

Wat ghelieft v heer oom

                  Die oom

Hoort kint slaet mijnder woorden goom
Ghi moet nae nimmeghen nemen v vertreck

The True and Very Strange Story of Mary of Nijmegen Who Lived for More than Seven Years with the Devil and Kept Company with Him.

Prologue

In the days when Duke Arnold of Gelderland was imprisoned by his son Duke Adolf and his accomplices in the city of Grave, there lived about three miles outside of Nijmegen a pious priest by the name of Master Gisbrecht. With him lived a beautiful young girl named Mary, his niece, whose mother was dead. The girl kept her uncle's household honestly and diligently.

¶ How Master Gisbrecht Sent His Niece Mary to Nijmegen.

It so happened that Master Gisbrecht wanted to send his niece Mary shopping for what they needed in the city of Nijmegen, saying to her:

{Woodcut A}

Uncle

Mary!

Mary

What would you like, Uncle?

Uncle
Now listen, child, and pay attention to what I say. You will have to go to Nijmegen and buy

Om ons prouande te halen wi hebbens ghebreck
Van keersen van olie in die lampe te doene
Van azine van soute ende van enzoene
En[de] van solferpriemen soe ghi selue ontcnoopt
Daer zijn acht stuuers gaet henen coopt
Te nimmeghen van dies wt² hebben breke
Tesser nv iuyst mertdach vander weke
Te bat suldi vinden al dat v ghereyt

    Mariken

Heer oom tot uwer onderdanscheit
Kent mi bereet in alder onderdanicheyt

    Die oom

Om tauont weder thuys te sine werdet te late
Want die daghen zijn seer cort nv ter wilen
En[de] tes van hier te nieumeghen twe groote mile[n]
En[de] tes nv tien vren of daer toe bet
Hoort kint eest dat ghier so langelet
Dat v dunct dat ghi met schonen daghe
Niet gheraken en sout tuwen behaghe
Blijft daer vri te nacht ick werts te gherustere

{A3ʳ}
En[de] gaet slapen tot uwer moeyen mijnder suster
Die en sal v om eenen nacht niet ontsegghen
Ick hebt lieuer dan dat ghidoer haeghe[n] en[de] hegge[n]
Thuys by doncker sout comen alleene
Want den wech en es van bouen niet alte reene
En[de] ghi sijt een schone ionghe lustighe maecht
Men soude v lichtelijck aenspreken

    Mariken

Heer oom soot v behaecht
So sal ick alle dinghen doen en[de] niet el

provisions. We need candles and oil for the lamp, vinegar, salt and onions. And matches, as you said yourself. Here are eight pennies. Go and buy what we need in Nijmegen. Today happens to be this week's market day. It will be quite easy to find everything you want.

Mary

Dear Uncle, you know I am happy to obey you.

Uncle

It's already getting too late to get home again before evening. The days are really short at this time of year, and from here to Nijmegen is a good two miles. It's already ten o'clock or maybe even later. Listen, child. If you think you can't return home easily in daylight, then stay there overnight. It would ease my mind. Go and sleep at your aunt's house. My sister won't refuse you for one night. I'd like that better than you coming home in the dark, walking alone through the countryside. The roads are unsafe because of outlaws, and you are a merry, beautiful young girl. You could very easily be attacked.

Mary

I'll do everything you say, Uncle, and nothing else.

Mariken van Nieumeghen / Mary of Nijmegen

Die oom

Geoet³ mi v moeye mijn suster en[de] vaert wel
Coopt al dat ons ghebrect bi mate en[de] bi gewichten

Mariken

Ick sal heer oom adieu

Die oom

Adieu mariken nichte
Gods gratie moet v een paer wesen
Heere godt hoe mach mi therte so swaer wesen
eest dattet lant hier so tweedrachtich si
Of eest om dat mijn nichte daer scheyt van mi
Ontbcyt hoe coem ic aldus swaer dits vree[m]t bediet
Met dat meysken daer van mi schiet
Wert mi te moede recht ick en weet hoe
Ick duchte haer oft mi sal wat comen toe
Ick wilde dat icse thuys hadde ghehouwen
Tes dwaesheit ionghe meyskens of vrouwen
Alleene te latengaen achter lande
Want die boeuerie der werelt is menigerhande

{A3ʳ} Aiij

{Woodcut B}

¶ Hoe mariken seer schandelijcken toe ghesproke[n] / wert van haerder moeyen

Aldus es mariken van haer heer oom ghescheide[n] / ende tot nieumeghen gegae[n] daer si cochte van als / dat haer oft haren oom nootelijc wesen mochte En[de] / opten seluen dach dat si te nimmeghen comen was / so hadde haer moeye teghens vier oft vijf vrouwe[n] / ghekeuen om des hertoghen adlof⁴ wille die synen / vader hadde doen vanghen als dat si bat schee[n] dul / oft een verwoede duyuelinne te sine dan een ker/sten mensche want si metten ionghen hertoge per/tijde ende vermoorde namaels
{A4ʳ}
Haer seluen doen si hoorde dat dye oude hertoghe / wter gheuanckenissen

Uncle

Give my sister my regards. Goodbye! And be sure to have everything we need weighed and measured correctly.

Mary

I will, Uncle. Goodbye!

Uncle

Goodbye, Mary, my Niece! May God's grace be with you!
Lord God, why is my heart so heavy? Is it because the country around here is in such turmoil? Or is it because my niece there is leaving me? Well! Why do I suddenly feel so sad? This is very strange! Just as that girl there left me, a strange feeling came over me. I felt as if something bad might happen to her or to me. I wish I had kept her at home. It's foolish to let young girls or women roam alone around the country, for the world is full of wickedness.

¶ How Mary Was Addressed by Her Aunt in A Most Contemptuous Manner.

Thus Mary parted from her uncle and went to Nijmegen, where she bought everything that she and her uncle needed. And on that same day, when Mary came to Nijmegen, her aunt had had a fight with four or five women on account of Duke Adolf, who had imprisoned his father, so that she seemed to be crazy or more like a raging she-devil than a Christian, because she sided with the young Duke. As you will hear, the Aunt killed herself later on when she heard that the old Duke had been released from prison

{Woodcut B}

verlost was bi toe done va[n] / den casteleyn vande[n] graue ghelijck ghi hier
na ho/ren sult Mariken siende dat biden auonde was als / si haer dinghen al
ghedaen hadde doe si om comen / was seide tot haer seluen aldus

    Nv heb ic van als dat ons ghebrack
    Doen weghen en[de] meten naer mijn ghemack
    Ende daer na ghecocht ende wel betaelt
    Maer mi dunct dat ic hier so langhe hebt[5] gedraelt
    Dat ghinder die nacht compt op gheresen
    Daer sie ick eenen wiser wat macht wesen
    Aenden dach tes alre tusschen vieren en[de] viuen
    Nv moet ic tauont int stede bliuen
    Ten es noch maer een vre dach
    En[de] in drie vren dat ict nauwelijck gaen en mach
    Va[n] hier tot mijns ooms neen tes beter ghebleue[n]
    Mijn moeye die woeut[6] recht hier neuen
    Ick wil haer gaen bidden datse mi een bedde decke
    En[de] morghen also vroech als ick ontwecke
    Doe mach ic mi nae huys snel ten labuere saen[7]
    Ick sie mijn moeye voer haer dore staen
    Soot wel betaemt wil icse gaen groeten
    Moeye cristus wil al v leet versoeten
    En[de] alle die ghi lief hebt hoeden van gequelle

            Die moeye

    Ke willecome duuel hoe staget in die helle
    Wel ioncfrouwe wat hebdi nv hier te doene

            Mariken

    Mijn oom sant mi omtrent der noene
    Om keersen om mostaert om azijn om veriuys
    En[de] om al datter ghebreck was tonsent in huys
    En[de] eer ick va[n] deen totte[n] anderen heb conne[n] loope[n]
    En[de] alledinck heb connen vinden ende coopen
    So eest sus late worden en[de] luttel grieuet v
    Dat ghi mi te nacht een bedde decket ghelieuet v
    Ic soude immer noch thuys gae[n] maer mett[er] nacht

by the caretaker of the city of Grave. Mary, having finished buying everything for which she had come, noticed that it was getting on toward evening and she said to herself:

Mary

Now I've bought everything we need to my satisfaction. I've had everything properly weighed and measured and paid the right amount of money. But it seems to me that I stayed too long. Already night is approaching. There's a sundial! What time is it? It's already between four and five! Now I'll have to stay in the city for the night. There is only one more hour of daylight, and it takes me at least three hours from here to my uncle's house. No! It's better to stay here. My aunt lives close by. I'll go and ask if she'll give me a bed. And tomorrow, as soon as I get up, I'll go home as quickly as possible and get back to work. I see my aunt standing in front of her door. I'll go and greet her politely.
Aunt, may Christ ease all your suffering and protect all your loved ones from harm!

Aunt

Oh Christ! Welcome, devil! How's it going in hell? Well, young lady, what are you doing here?

Mary

Around noon my uncle sent me for candles, mustard, vinegar and verjuice for cooking, and everything we need at home. And before I could run from one store to the next and find and buy everything, it had gotten this late. I hope it won't be too much trouble for you to make me a bed for the night, if you'd be so kind. I could still go home, but a girl is

Wort somtijts een maechdeke[n] bespiet en[de] gewacht
Onteert vercracht te haren verwite
Ende daer voer sorghe ick

Die moeye

Wachermen tijte
Sorchdi nv so seere voor uwe[n] machdo[m] godwouds
Ke lieue nichte ghi weet doch van oudts
Hoe ghi ghewonnen waert al ghelaeti v dus inge
Ghi enhebt hier sint der noenen met uwen dinge
Niet besich gheweest laet ic mi duncken

Mariken

Ick doe seker moeye

Die moeye

Ja oft sitten drincken
Iewers int heimelijke nae ws herten willeken
Ke nichte te lande waert cleyken ende gilleke[n]
Connen alte wel dese meyskens int coren leyde[n]
En[de] alse ten auontspele gaen onder hem beyden
Hoe wort lijse dan van hannen ghetoest[8]
Ke nichte ghi hebtet al wel gheproeft
Want touwent woont so menich frisch gheselleke[n]

Mariken

Twy segdi dat moeye

{A5ʳ}

Die moeye

Ey dobbel velleken
Al en dooch die waerheyt niet gheseyt
Ghy hebt menighen rey ghereyt
Daer die pijper geen vijf groote en wan

sometimes waylaid at night, ambushed and then raped and ruined. That's what I worry about.

Aunt

Oh my! You poor babe! Are you so worried about your virginity now? By God, if that were only true! Christ, dear Niece, for a long time you have known how you were bred, even if you now pretend to be so afraid. And I don't believe you've been busy shopping here since noon!

Mary

I certainly have, Aunt!

Aunt

Indeed! Or sat around somewhere secretly drinking to your heart's content. Christ, Niece, in the country Nick and Bill know only too well how to take girls into the cornfields; and when the two of them go and play their evening games with each other, oh, how Jill is petted by Jack! Christ, Niece, you've already tried that yourself, with so many horny guys living out your way.

Mary

Why are you saying this, Aunt?

Aunt

You cunning little hussy! Even if it's indecent to tell the truth, you yourself have danced many a dance for which the piper didn't get paid with money!

En[de] al gaetmen langhe af ende an
Tes al maecht tot dat den buyck op rijst

Mariken

Dat ghi mi dese scande bewijst
Sonder schult eest mi te hert om verdraghen

Die moye[9]

Ick hebbe lieden ghesproken dye v lestent saghen
Met uwen eygene[n] oom ligghen so ontscamelijck
Dat mi te segghen waer om betamelijck
Onteeren blamelijck doedi al ons geslachte
Tfij moet v worden onsalighe drachte
Ick en mach v niet sien te mijnen goede

Mariken

Here god hoe wee wert mi te moede
Hoe ontstelt van bloede
Werdt mijn gheheel lichaem soudeynich
Die smedige woorden dit verwijt vileynich
Te hoorene en[de] te verdragen sonder schult
Nv moeye segt oft ghi mi een bedde decken sult
Desen nacht ende niet langher

Die moeye

Ghi laecht mi lieuer in die maze
Alsoe diepe als dit huys hooch is tot eenen aze
Van alle die visschen dier inne vlieten
Dus vertrect van hier oft het sal v verdrieten

{A5ᵛ}

Van thoorne sta ick als een loof en beue

Mariken

Moeye ghi hebt groot onghelijck

And even if you've been practicing how to move up and down for a long time already, you're all virgins until your belly swells.

Mary

I can't bear to listen to these shameful accusations you heap on me without reason.

Aunt

I talked with people who saw you not long ago sleeping so shamelessly with your uncle that it would be indecent of me to speak of it. It's outrageous, how you're disgracing our whole family. Shame on you, you evil creature! I can't bear to look at you!

Mary

Dear Lord, suddenly I feel so terrible! My whole body feels drained of blood. To have to listen to these contemptuous words! To have to bear this vile accusation without deserving it! Now, Aunt, tell me, will you give me a bed for the one night?

Aunt

I'd rather see you lie as deep in the river Maas as this house is high, as bait for all the fish swimming around in it. Get out of here or you'll be sorry! I am standing here trembling like a leaf from anger!

Mary

Aunt, you are doing me a grave injustice!

Die moeye

Ontbeyt dese verhide teue
En sal mi niet late[10] nonghequelt[11]
Moeten die tuyten wat zijn verstelt
Ia si beghint mi den worm int hoot te roerene
Ick stae quaet ghenoch om den duuel te snoerene
Oft om op een cussen te binden al waer hi kintsch
Ic stae wel soe spijtelijcken en wensch
Ic en weet nauwe ofic op my[n] hoot sta of my[n] voete[n]
Alle die mi desen dach ontmoeten
Die sal ick antwoerden dwelck mi dit beroer doet
Alleens ghelijck die duuel zijn moer doet

Mariken

O bedructe nv is v lijden naest
Ick bliue staende wel so beraest
Dat ick van miseluen en weet hoe noch wat
Met eenen dullen hoofde loop ic noch wter stat
Ontsiende boeuen noch daer toe roouers
Ic scatte ic mijn bedde make onder die loouers
Ic en vrage na niemant die nv leuende si
Al quaem die baerlijcke duuel tot mi
Ic ben nv als die nieghers nae en vraghe
Nv gae ic sitten onder dese haghe
Mi seluen beuelende inden handen
Van gode of alle die helsche vianden

¶ Hoe Mariken van haerder moeyen schiet ende / wt Nieumeghen ghinck
{A6ʳ}
Aldus es die ionghe maecht marike[n] van haerder / moeyen gescheyde[n] ende al weenende seer mestroe/stich metten donckeren auont wter stadt van nieu-/meghen ghegaen so langhe dat si quam neuens ee[n] / groote dicke haghe daer si met grooten drucke on- /der ghinck sitten weenen ende screyen haer seluen / den viant seer dicwils ouerghevende met droeuer / herten tot haer seluen segghende aldus

Weemi suchten crijsschen en[de] hant ghewrinck
Mi seluen hetende vermalendijt
Dats nv mijn solaes en[de] anders gheen dinck

Aunt

Well, this damn bitch won't leave me alone! Do I have to tear off your pigtails? Yes, she's driving me crazy! I'm mad enough to wrestle with the devil and tie him to a pillow as if he were a baby. I stand here shaking with rage! I don't know if I'm coming or going. I'm in such a foul mood I'll talk to everyone I meet today just like the devil bitches at his mother.

Mary

Oh, poor, wretched me! Now suffering is upon me. I stand here so completely beside myself that I don't know myself, nor how, nor what. Numb and dazed, I'll run out of town, not even fearing rapists or robbers. I think I'll make my bed under these branches. I don't care about anyone, even if the devil himself should appear before me. I feel myself abandoned and I don't care about anything. Now I'll go and sit under this hedge and commend myself into the hands of God or all the devils in hell.

¶ How Mary Departed from Her Aunt and Left Nijmegen.

Thus, the young girl Mary departed from her aunt, crying and in despair, and left the city of Nijmegen in the dark of night until she came to a large, thick thorn-bush where she sat down, very dejected, weeping and wailing, again and again commending herself with a wretched heart to the devil, saying to herself:

Mary

Alas! I moan! I wail! I wring my hands! I call myself cursed! That's now my only consolation and nothing else!

Doer mijns moeyen scandch[12] verwijt
Eest onrecht dattet mi spijt
Sonder cause sulcken woorden te lijden
Neent vri in mi groeit sulcken nijt
Daer therte in wast nv talder tijt
Dat ic quaet ghenoech sitte in dit berijt
Om mi seluen eewich te vermalendien
Hulpe welcken temptacie comt mi bespringhen
Wil ic mi seluen verhanghen oft craghen
O ioncheyt suldi v connen bedwinghen
Oft en wildi nae gheen reden vraghen
Wie soude oock alsulcken woorden verdraghen
Sonder schult hi en is niet leuende ic meens
Diese sonder verdiente wel soude behaghen
Dies segick in wanhopen die mi comt belagen
Comt nv tot mi ende mi beclaghen
God of die duuel tes mi alleleens

{A6ᵛ}
{Woodcut C}

DIe viant die altijt zijn stricke[n] en[de] netten spreit / Haecke[n]de nae die verdoemenis der siele[n] dese / woorden hoore[n]de seyde tot he[m] seluen aldus

Dat woert werdt mi die siele weerdich
Ick hebbe mi seluen toeghemaect rechtueerdich
Al waer ick een mensche en[de] al bi gods ghedooghe
Tes al te passe sonder mijn een oghe
Die is of si mi wt waer ghesworen
Wi gheeste[n] en hebben dye macht niet dats verlore[n]
Ons te volmakenne doer gheen bespreck

Is it wrong that I am so deeply offended by my aunt's insulting slander, for having to listen to such accusations without cause? Certainly not! I feel growing within myself such bitterness that it fills my heart more and more. This violent attack of feelings drives me toward such wickedness that I'm ready to throw myself into eternal perdition. My God! What temptation assails me? Do I really want to throw myself away or even cause my own death? Oh child, won't you control yourself and listen to reason? But who'd be able to suffer such words without feeling guilty? I believe no one would like to hear them without having deserved them! I say this in total despair assailing me. Now come and pity me, be it God or the devil, it's all the same to me!

{Woodcut C}

The devil, who always sets his snares and traps, wanting the damnation of souls, said to himself when he heard these words:

The Devil

This speech makes this soul valuable to me. I have dressed myself up just right to appear exactly like a human being! And that even with God's permission! It's all been arranged very nicely; except for my one eye. It looks as if I'd lost it because of an infection. We spirits no longer have the power to make our appearance perfect with the help of some sort of

Altoos es aen ons eenich ghebreck
Tsi aen thoot aen handen oft aen voeten

Nv willick mijn voiseken wat gaen versoeken[13]
ende spreken so weluallende en[de] met beschede
Dat ick mijnen bloe[14] niet en verseede[15]
Ten eerste[n] salme[n] die die[16] vrouwe[n] soetelijc ouergae[n]
Schoon kint hoe sitti dus beschaemt
Heft v yemant mesdaen
Sonder redene ofte recht
Dat sal ick wreken als een goet knecht
Ghi dunct mi slecht
Ende daer omme sicick[17] ick
Hier tuwen trooste

Mariken

Hulp god hoe verscrick ick
Wat mijns ick en weet van mi seluen nauwelijck
Met dat ick dien me[n]sche ben aenschuwelijck[18]
Hulpe hoe flauwelijck verualt mi therte

Die duuel

Schoon kint en vreest grief noch smerte
Ick en sal v hindere grief noch quaet doen
Maer ick gheloue v wildi na mijnen raet doen
Ende met mi gaen wilt dit onthouden nauwe
Ick make v eer lanc der vrouwen vrauwe

Mariken

Vrient ick sitte nv rechs also ghesint
So beroert en[de] soo ontstelt van engienen
Doer die schimpighe woerde[n] die ic sonder v[er]dine[n]
Heb moeten lijden hoere schueke ende teue
Dies ic mi alsoe lief den viant ouergheue
Als gode want ick sitte half sonder sin

incantation. That power has been lost. There always must be some sort of deformity either of the head, the hands or feet. Now I'll practice my sweet-talk and speak so pleasantly and nicely that I won't offend my darling. At the start one must speak sweetly to women.
Beautiful child, why do you sit there so dejected? Did someone hurt you for no reason and without any cause? I will avenge it as your faithful servant. You seem so innocent to me. That's why, for your consolation, I put myself at your disposal.

Mary

Oh God, how frightened I am! What does this mean? Since I've been looking at this man, I hardly know myself! Oh God, how weak my heart is getting!

The Devil

Beautiful child! You mustn't be afraid that I will hurt you or cause you any pain! I'll cause you no sorrow, grief or harm. But I swear to you, if you follow my advice, carry out my instructions exactly and come with me, before long I'll make you the most distinguished lady in the world.

Mary

Friend, I have good reason to sit here in such a state. I am enraged and completely beside myself because of insults heaped upon me without any reason: whore, slut and bitch! That's why I am just as ready to surrender myself to the devil as to God, because I am sitting here half out of my mind.

Die duuel

Bi lucifer tes noch al ghewin
Si heeft de beroerte te deghe op ghespogen[19]
Si sit noch euen versteent in wanhopen
Nv soudic hopen te min so claech ic nv
Dat ic niet missen en sal scoo[n] kint noch vraech ick v
Oft ghi met mi versamen wilt in ionsten

Mariken

Wie sidi vrient

Die duuel

Een meester vol consten
Nieuwers af falende wes ic besta

Mariken

Tcomt mi alleleens met wien dat ick ga
Also lief gae ic mette[n] quaetsten als metten beste[n]

Die duuel

Wildi v liefde te mi werts vesten
Ick sal v consten leeren sonder ghelijcke
Die seuen vrie consten rethorijcke musijcke
Logica gramatica ende geometrie
Aristmatica ende alkenie[20]
Dwelc al consten sijn seer curable
Noyt vrouwe en leefde op eerde so able
Als ic v maken sal

Mariken

So moetti wel zijn een constich man
Wie sidi dan

The Devil

By Lucifer, this is of great advantage to me!
She is completely absorbed in her own
confusion. There she sits, petrified in her
despair. I've really got nothing to complain
about! I can hope now that I won't fail.
Beautiful child, I ask you again, will you join
me in love and affection?

Mary

Who are you, friend?

The Devil

A master of many arts, who never fails in
anything he tries.

Mary

I don't care with whom I go. I'm just as happy
to go with the most evil person in the world as
with the best.

The Devil

If you agree to join me in a union of love, I'll
teach you incomparable skills; the seven liberal
arts: rhetoric, music, logic, grammar and
geometry, arithmetic and alchemy, all of which
are highly respected. No other woman on earth
before was ever as clever as I'll make you.

Mary

Well, then you must be indeed a talented man.
Who are you?

####### Die duuel

Wat leyt v daer an
Wie ick ben en soudi met rechte vraghen niet

{B2ʳ}

Ick en ben die beste van mijnen maghen niet
Maer v dat ic emmermeer niet dan ionste en toge

####### Mariken

Hoe heeti vrient

####### Die duuel

Moenen metter eender ooghe
Die wel bekent es met veel goede ghesellen

####### Mariken

Ghi sijt die viant vander hellen

####### Die duuel

Wie ick ben ic ben emmer gheionstich tot v

####### Mariken

Ick en hebbe oeck van v ancxt vrese noch gru
Al quame luycefer selue wter helscher ghewelt
Ick en souder niet af veruaert sijn so ben ic gestelt
Ick ben onghequelt van allen anxten

####### Die duuel

Ia schoenkint dits tcorste ende dlancxte
Wildi m[et] my gae[n] en[de] mijne[n] raet doen sonder veyse[n]
Al dat ghi dincken moecht oft peysen
Sal ick v leeren soe ick v eerst vertelde
Van goede van iuwelen noch van ghelde
En suldi ooc nemmermeer hebben ghebrec

The Devil

What do you care? There are good reasons why you shouldn't ask me who I am. I am not the best member of my family; but never mind, I'll never show you anything but affection.

Mary

What's your name, friend?

The Devil

One-eyed Moenen, who is well acquainted with a large company of merry party-goers.

Mary

You are the fiend of hell!

The Devil

No matter who I am, I'll always be kind to you.

Mary

I'm not afraid of you; nor do I feel in any danger nor feel any aversion toward you. Even if Lucifer himself should appear from the kingdom of hell, I wouldn't be frightened. That's how I am! I feel myself free of all fears.

The Devil

Indeed, beautiful child! But now to the point: do you want to come with me and follow all my instructions without question? As I promised you before, I'll teach you anything you can imagine or dream. And you'll never have to go without riches, jewels and money.

Mariken

Tes wel gheseyt maer nae deerste bespreck
Eer ghi met mi sult versamen iu[21] ionsten
Suldi mi leeren die seuen vrie consten
Want in alle dinghen te leeren verfray ick
Ghi sullet mi al leeren suldi

{B2ᵛ}

Die duuel

Wat trouwen ia ick
Ick sal v leeren al dat wel voechlijck is

Mariken

Nigremansie dats een const die ghenoechelijck es
Mijn oom es daer af vael ende clocck
Hy maect wo[n]der somtijts hi heefter af eene[n] boeck
Ick wane hi hem in node noyt en faelde
Hi soude door die ooghe van eender naelde
Den viant wel doen cruypen teghen sinen danck
Die conste moetti mi oock leeren

Die duuel

O aenschijn blanck
Al wes ick can v seluen verfoyt[22]
Es al om v maer ick en leerde noyt
Niegermansie daer veele aencleeft
Tes een conste die veel moyten heeft
Ende daer oock vele sorgheu[23] inne steeck[24]
Als ghi nigermansie begint en[de] v ontbreeckt
Een woort oft een letter schoon rode mondt
Ende ghi den gheest die ghi roept ter stont
Niet en cont beuelen ofte passe spreken
Hi soude v ter stont den necke breken
Dus leiter groot grief inne scoon edel bloeme

Mary

That's all very well! But before I join you in a loving union, you'll have to teach me the seven liberal arts, just as you first promised. Because I'd love to learn everything. You will teach me, won't you?

The Devil

Indeed, just as I promised! I'll teach you everything that's proper!

Mary

Necromancy is a pleasant art! My uncle knows a lot about it and is very clever at it. He has a book about it. Sometimes he makes miracles happen. I don't think he ever failed in it when he needed help. He could make the devil, against his will, crawl through the eye of a needle. You'll have to teach me that art, too!

The Devil

Oh, my pretty angel! Everything I know is at your disposal. Just to make you happy! But I've never really learned necromancy, which is very complicated. It's a very difficult art involving many dangers. My sweet darling, if you begin a spell in necromancy and the spirit you called appears, and you don't address him with the proper words, or you are unable to control him instantly because you missed a word or even a single letter, he could immediately break your neck. You see, my pretty little flower, there's a lot of trouble associated with it.

Mariken

Eest so soe en gheef icker dan niet omme
Ick en wil niet leeren daer ic bi sou moghen sneue[n]

Die duuel

Ha ha dat heb ic haer ontgheuen
Wat sou si nighermancie begheeren te leeren

{B3ʳ}

Cost si nighermancie twaer om te verseerne
Ende tot haren accoort te keerne
Die gheheel helle ende te brenghen in laste
En[de] tware om mi te bedwinghen alst haer paste
Oft mi yewers te legghen vaste
Daer ic en soude moghen noch wech noch van
Haer nigherma[n]cie te leere[n] daer en comc ic niet an
Do ick best can
Sal ick haer dat houden wten sinne
Hoort wat ic v noch leeren sal mijn schoone minne
Om dat ghi die nighermancie sout laten varen

Mariken

Wat suldi noch leeren

Die duuel

Dat sal ick v verclaren
Alle die talen der werelt sal ick v leeren
So sal v alle die werelt verheffen ende eeren
Wa[n]t alle die talen te connen ghi en weet n[iet] wat si
Ende dan die seuen vri consten daer bi
Tes om van elcke[n] verheue[n] te sijn seer excelle[n]telijc

Mariken

Daenhoren vesacht minen druck tormentelijck
Gheheel obedientelijck
Stel ick mi touwen wille en[de] ghijt so doet

Mary

If that's the case, I don't want any part of it. I don't want to learn anything which could harm me.

The Devil

Ha, ha, I've talked her out of that! What an idea, wanting to learn necromancy! If she knew necromancy, she'd be a real nuisance for us, subject all of hell to her will and cause us a lot of trouble. She could also control me whenever she felt like it. Or she could even tie me up somehow, so I wouldn't be able to get loose and escape. Teach her necromancy? I wouldn't touch it! I'll talk her out of it as best I can.
Since you'll have to give up necromancy, listen to what else I'll teach you, my lovely beauty.

Mary

What else will you teach me?

The Devil

Let me explain! I'll teach you all the languages of the world. Then the whole world will praise and honor you. You don't know what it means to be able to speak all those languages! And along with all those languages you'll know the seven liberal arts. You'll indeed be praised by everyone in the most glowing terms.

Mary

Listening to all of this makes me feel a lot less depressed. I submit voluntarily and obediently to your will, if you keep your promises.

####### Die duuel

Maer een bede sal ic aen v begheren beelde soet
En ghi mi dit doet het sal v wel baten

####### Mariken

Wat beden es datte

{B3ᵛ}   Biij
####### Die duuel

Dat ghi uwen naem soudt willen laten
En[de] geue[n] v seluen eene[n] andere[n] nae[m] van nv voort ae[n]
Mariken es voer mi een ombequaem woort
Bi ee[n]der marie[n] ic en[de] mij[n] geselscap sulc grief hebbe[n]
Dat wi nemmermeer dien nae[m] en sulle[n] lief hebbe[n]
Doet doch v seluen lijnke[n] grietke[n] of lyske[n]
noemen
Ick beloue v eer dat iaer lijt het sal v vromen
Meer dan ghi noyt hadt van vrienden oft magen

####### Mariken

Ey lacen twi mach v dien naem meshaghen
Tes doch den edelsten en[de] den soetsten naeme
Van alle der werelt en[de] elcken bequame
Marike[n] oft maria hoe moechdi dien naem weten
Om al dat leeft en wille ic anders niet heten
Mi dunct men mach dien naem niet versoeten

####### Die duuel

Ey ey nv es mijn werck weder al o[n]der die voeten
Can ick desen naem niet doen veranderen
Hoort lief willen wi wandelen met malcanderen
Soe moetti uwen naem verandere[n] al deret v seer

The Devil

But there's one more request I must ask of you, my sweet angel. If you agree to it, I promise it'll be to your advantage.

Mary

And what is that?

The Devil

That you give up your name and from now on call yourself something else. "Mary" is an unpleasant name for me. My companions and I have already had a lot of trouble with one Mary; we'll never have much appreciation for that name. Why don't you call yourself Lynnie, Peggy or Lizzy? I promise you, before a year has gone by, it will benefit you more than anything you ever got from your family or your friends.

Mary

Oh, but why should you dislike that name? After all, it is the sweetest, most noble name in the whole world, and everyone finds it delightful. Mary or Maria. How did you know my name? By all that lives, I don't want to be called anything else. I don't think there is a sweeter name.

The Devil

Oh damn! If I can't get her to change that name, all my hard work has again gone for nothing. Listen, my love, if we're going to keep company with each other, no matter how much you dislike it, you'll have to change your name.

Oft wi moeten scheyden en[de] voort noch meer
Moetti mi belouen peyst belofte es schult

                Mariken

Wat sal ick belouen

                Die duuel

Dat ghi v nemmermeer seghenen en sult
Wat dat v toe compt oft pijnt te deerne
Ghi en moecht v niet seghenen

{B4ʳ}

                Mariken

Dat beloue ick v gheerne
Aent segghen en leyt mi niet veel an
Maer minen naem ick qualic gheloechenen can
Want maria daer ic naer hete dats alle mij[n] troost
Mijn hope want alsi mi yet grief of noost
Roep ic ter stont op haer om een beuredinghe
Oeck dien icxse daghelicx met eender bedinghe
Die ic van ioncx hebbe gheleert
Maria die wert van mi gheeert
Also lange als ic kennisse hebbe des niet en faelt
Al sla ic int milde[25] of al regeer ic mi qualic
Haer te louen en mach niet zijn vergheten

                Die duuel

Nv om dat ghi so seer sijt veruleten
Op dien name hoort ic sal v noch beghere[n] nettere
Ick ben te vreden dat ghi hout deerste settere[26]
Van uwen name vrou ongheblaemt fijn
Dats de .m. dus suldi Emmeken genaemt sijn
In v lant sijn doch veel maechden ende vrouwen
Die emmeken ghenaemt sijn

Or we'll have to go our separate ways! And you'll have to promise me something else, too. Remember, a promise is a promise!

Mary

What else do I have to promise?

The Devil

That, no matter what happens, no matter what kind of trouble you find yourself in, you'll never again bless yourself by making the sign of the cross. You must never make the sign of the cross again.

Mary

I'm happy to promise you that! I don't care very much about making the sign of the cross; but I can hardly deny my own name! After all, the Virgin Mary, for whom I was named, is all my hope and comfort. Whenever something bothers me or hurts me, I quickly turn to her for comfort. I also pray to her every day with a prayer I have known since childhood. No, I've worshipped the Virgin Mary for as long as I can remember. I'll never fail to do that, even if I turn wild and behave shamefully. I'll never forget to worship her!

The Devil

All right, since you are so fond of that name, listen, I'll compromise. I'll be satisfied if you keep only the first letter of your name, my exquisite, gentle lady! That's the letter "M"; that's why you'll be called Emily! After all, there are many girls and women in your country called Emily.

Mariken

Nv wel moenen mach ic niet behouwen
Mine[n] rechten name lyeuer²⁷ dan wi scheede[n] souwe[n]
So ben ic metter eerster letter te vreden
Emmeken sal ic heeten tallen steden
Nochtans en doe icx niet gheerne

Die duuel

Sijt segt ghepayt
Ent niet al op uwen duym en drayt

{B4ᵛ}

Eer een iaer doeges mi verwijt
Gae wi na tshertoghen bossche sonder respijt
Ende van daer en werd ons gheen ruste
Wi en comen tantwerpen na onsen luste
Daer wert een wonder van ons begonnen
Eer wi daer comen suldi alle die talen connen
Die ghi begheert te leerene soe ick v seyde
Ende die zeuen vrije consten tot uwen geeste
Bastaert malueseye wert uwen eertschen²⁸ dra[n]ck
Cond mijn vrientscap houden en[de] minen danck
Tes wonder wat ghi noch sult bedrijuen
Maer ten eynde hope ick salder v siele bliuen

Nae dese woorden zijn emmeken en[de] moenen nae / des hertoghen bosche ghereyst daer si sommighe / dage[n] bleue[n] teere[n]de seer rijckelijc voer ee[n] yegelijcke[n] / betaelden die met hem lyeden qua[m] eten oft drincke[n]

¶ Nv sellen wy een luttel swighen van emmeken / ende moenen ende bescriuen va[n] heer Ghijsbrecht / Emmekens oom

NA dat marike[n] dyemen nv emmeken noemt / sommighe daghen wech geweest hadde soe / was heer ghijsbrecht haer oom seer verwonderdt / van haer langhe bliue[n] segge[n]de tot he[m] seluen aldus

O murmeracie die mi al euen stranghe creyt
Hoe ontstelt ghi hert sin ende verstant

Mary

Well, all right, Moenen, if I can't keep my own name, I'll be satisfied with the first letter. That's better than having to leave you. From now on I shall be known everywhere as Emily, even if I don't like it.

The Devil

Listen, you should be satisfied! If, after one year everything hasn't turned out exactly as you wish, you may hold me accountable. Now, without further delay, let's be off to the city of 's-Hertogenbosch, and from there we'll move on to Antwerp at our leisure. We'll do unbelievable things! Before we arrive there, you'll be able to speak all those languages you wanted to learn, just as I told you; and you'll have mastered the seven liberal arts. Sweet domestic wine and even sweet Greek wine will be your daily drink. It will be marvelous, the wonderful things you'll be able to do!
And in the end, I hope, your soul will be lost.

After this conversation Emily and Moenen traveled to the city of s-Hertogenbosch, where they remained for several days, living in luxury, paying the bill for anyone who ate and drank with them.

¶ Now We Will Be Silent for A While about Emily and Moenen
and Write about Master Gisbrecht, Emily's Uncle.

After Mary, who is now called Emily, had been gone for several days, Master Gisbrecht was very much disturbed by her long absence, saying to himself:

Uncle

Oh, disturbing premonitions, which clamor louder and louder for my attention! How you trouble my heart, my soul, my mind!

Om dat mariken mijn nichte soe langhe beyt
Die ick om prouande te nimmeghen sant
Ick seyde haer nochtan quaem die nacht op hant
Ofte datse haer veruaerde in eenigher wiijs
Dat si tot mijn susters soude gaen slapen want

{C1ʳ}

Als ick te nimmeghe[n] come dats altoos mij[n] logijs
Ick en hebbe hert sin noch auijs
Ick en moet weten hoet met haer staet
Mesquaem haer iet doer eenich afgrijs
Ick storue sonder hope of troost
Want tmeysken is alle mijn toeuerlaet
En[de] van ioncx heb icse op ghehouwen
Dus soude icker aensien node eenich quaet
Maer seer lichte vertwifeltmen ionge vrouwen
Dit es nae nimmeghen sonder vercouwen
Om van haer te hooren recht bescheet
Sulck hoort somtijts tes hem om hooren leet

Nae desen woorden is heer ghijsbrecht tot zijns su/sters huys gegaen haer vragende na marike[n] haer/der beyder nichte dye welcke seer straffelijck andt/woerde dat si van haer niet en wiste Waero[m] hi seer / droeue was tot haer seggende aldus

    Ey lazen suster ghi beguyt mi
    Dat ghi segt dat gi van maeyken niet en weet

              Die suster marikens moeye

    Ey neen ick seker goey ian dunct mi

              Die oom

    Ey lazen suster ghi beguyt mi

              Die moeye

    Ick schat si yeuers in een camer ghemuyst[29] si
    Daermen sulke[n] tijtke[n]s om een grootken speet

Because my niece Mary, whom I sent for provisions to Nijmegen, has been gone for such a long time. It's true, I told her that if night should fall or if she felt afraid in any way, she should go and sleep at my sister's house. Whenever I go to Nijmegen, that's where I always stay. I search my heart and soul for a way of finding out what's become of her. If some horrible calamity should have befallen her, I'd die in desolation and despair, because the girl is the only comfort I have. I raised her since childhood. I couldn't bear it if any harm came to her. But it's so easy to lead young women astray! I must go immediately to Nijmegen and make inquiries about her. But sometimes one hears what one doesn't want to hear!

After these words, Master Gisbrecht went to his sister's house, asking her about their niece Mary. But she answered very harshly that she knew nothing about her, and he became very dismayed and said to her:

Uncle

Oh, Sister, you're trying to make a fool of me
if you claim that you know nothing about Mary.

The Sister, Mary's Aunt

Well, I certainly do not, you poor sucker, you!

Uncle

Oh, Sister, you're trying to lie to me!

Aunt

I guess she is locked up somewhere in a room,
where for a few coins they impale such chicks
on a cock.

Die oom

Ey lazen suster ghi beguyt mi
Dat ghi segt dat ghi van haer niet en weet
Ghi ghelaet v verstoort en[de] seer tonureet
Om dat ic v come vraghen met woerde[n] saechtich
Oft ghise niet ghesien en hebt

Die moeye

dats seker warachtich
En ghelaet v al had icse te bewarene ghenomen
Tes acht oft tien daghen lede[n] dat si hier was come[n]
Segghende moeye dect mi een bedde desen nacht
Ic en derre niet thuys gae[n] oft ic ware gewacht
Van boeuen dye machdeke[n]s geerne mesuerghen
doen seide ic haer dat si sou gaen ter herberghen
daer si al den dach had sitten drincken en[de] scincken

Die oom

Hoe hadse al den dach sitten drincken

Die moeie[30]

dat moechdi wel dincken
dat si gheweest hadde daert haer niet en v[er]droot
Si quam hier met een kinnebacken also root
Als een eersgat met vuysten ghesleghe[n]
En[de] om dat ic daer wat seyde teghen
Tschee[n] datsi mi gheten sou hebbe[n] mette[n] mostaerde
Al vloecke[n]de en[de] al tiere[n]de lyepse haerder vaerde
En[de] noyt sint en heb ick mijn ioncfrouwe ghesien

Dye oom

Ey lazen wat sal mijns dan gheschien
O godheyt in drien
Waer sal dmeysen gheuaren zijn

Uncle

Alas, Sister, you're trying to mislead me if you claim that you know nothing about her. You have become very angry and aggravated just because I have come to ask you politely if you have seen her.

Aunt

That's true enough! And don't act as if it was my duty to take care of her! It was eight or ten days ago when she came here saying, "Aunt, give me a bed for tonight. I'm afraid to go home because I might be ambushed by thugs who like to abuse young girls." Then I told her to go back to the inn where she had been drinking and partying all day.

Uncle

What! Had she been drinking all day?

Aunt

You can bet that no matter where she was hanging out, she wasn't bored. She came here with her cheeks as red as a well-thrashed fanny. And just because I said something about it, she almost bit my head off! Then she ran off carrying on and cursing all the way. Since then I haven't seen the lady.

Uncle

Alas, what will become of me? Oh, dear God, where can the girl have gone?

Dye moeye

Ey goey yewers inden droeuen of claren wijn
daer si vergarende zijn
die de goey ghesellen deersgat leenen

{C2ʳ}

Dye oom

Ey lasen suster ghi doet mi weenen
Dat v alsulcke woerden ontuloten

Die moye[31]

Haddise in een cofferken ghesloten
So haddi moghen dit grief beweeren
Keren lief man wat salt haer deeren
Al machse wat ghebruycken haers willen
Ten sal haer een enckel mite niet schillen
Si en sals oeck niet te nauwer zijn een stro
Si en salder niet manck af gaen

Dye oom

Och ick hoore dit so no
dat mi therte dunct in vieren spliten
Ick moet omme keeren en[de] minen oghen witen
Want die tranen ontuallen mi lancx die caken
O moeder ons heeren die ick binnen aken
Alle iaer besoecke met ionsten deuotelijck
Staet mi nv bi het is mi notelijck
En[de] ghi sinte seruaes rustende binnen maestricht
die van mi tsiaers menich scoon licht
Wt deuocien wert ghestelt
Mi hoepic dat ghi niet beswijcken en selt
Ter noot salmen troost aen vrienden soecken
Ic wil gae[n] v[er]nemen en[de] doen v[er]neme[n] in alle hoeken
Ofter yemant af heeft ghehoort
Al ben ic ghestoort
Ten es gheen wondere dat mi tderue[n] grief gheeft
Niemant en scheet gheerne van dat hi liefheeft

{C2ᵛ}

Aunt

Why, my good man, somewhere in a wine shop where they get together to hire out their cunts to some lucky fellows!

Uncle

Oh, Sister, it makes me weep to hear you speak like that!

Aunt

You'd have been able to prevent such trouble only if you'd locked her up in a trunk. Jesus Christ, my dear man, what harm will it do her, even if she does tend to be a bit stubborn? It won't make a bit of difference to her and she won't be any the worse for it! She won't be crippled by it.

Uncle

Oh, I listen to this with such aversion that I feel as if my heart were breaking. I must turn away, ashamed of my eyes, for tears are running down my cheeks. Oh, Mother of God, whom I visit devotedly every year in Aachen, stand by me in my hour of need! And you, Saint Servatius, resting in Maastricht, to whom I have dedicated many a beautiful candle in devotion every year! I hope that you won't desert me. When in need, one should seek comfort from friends. I'll go now and investigate, inquire everywhere if anyone might have heard something about this. No wonder I'm so confused; missing her hurts me so much. Nobody likes to be separated from someone he loves.

Mariken van Nieumeghen / Mary of Nijmegen

¶ Na desen is heer ghijsbrecht van sijnder sustere[n] / ghescheyden met droeuen moede om dat hij geen / tijdinghe van mariken zijn nichte en verhoorde

{Woodcut D}

¶ Hoe marike[n]s moeye haer selue[n] dye kele af stack

BInnen desen middelen tijde heeft die casteley[n] / va[n]den graue den ouden hertoge .Arent wten / gheuanckenisse ghelaten hem leede[n]de in die stadt / van Shertoghen bossche daer hi seer feestelijc ont/fanghen was vanden heeren vander seluer stadt / Dwelcke dese marikens moeye hore[n]de wert daer / om so toornich in haer fenijnich herdt dat si naelicx / gheborsten hadde van quaetheden seggende
{C3ʳ}
    ¶ Hulpe leueren longeren en[de] milten
    Tanden hoofden wat ic al leets ghewinne
    Den spijt sal mi doen bersten of smilten
    Want ic swelle van quaetheyt als een spinne
    Verwoet dul werdt ic en[de] buyten sinne
    Doer die nieumere die ic daer hebbe verstaen
    Doude dief die te graue opt slot lach in die rinne
    Die is verlost en[de] laten gaen
    Och nv es alle mijnen troost ghedaen
    Want ons ionghe hertoghe bi wien ic bliue
    Sal nv ducht ick zijn hant opt bloote slaen
    Ick bender so inne beroert dat ic mi saen
    Ouer gheuen soude met siele met liue
    En[de] roepen alle duuels te mijnen verstiue

          Die duuel

Ha ha van dien bedriue
Soudic profijt hebben
Die siele es mijn mach ic den tijt hebben
Van een half vre ontrent haer te sine

Mariken van Nieumeghen / Mary of Nijmegen

¶ After this Master Gisbrecht Parted from His Sister with A Sad Heart Because He Had Not Heard Any News about His Niece Mary.

¶ How Mary's Aunt Cut Her Own Throat.

In the meantime, the chatelain of the city of Grave had freed old Duke Arent from prison and led him into the city of s'-Hertogenbosch where he was welcomed with a great celebration by the gentlemen of that city. When Mary's aunt heard about this she became so enraged in her malicious, evil heart that she almost burst from anger, saying:

{Woodcut D}

Aunt

By God's liver, belly and spleen, teeth and head! The pain I have to put up with! This anger will make me burst or burn me up. I've swollen up with evil like a spider. I'm beside myself, furious, raving mad, because of the news I've just heard! That old thief, who sat in jail in the castle of the city of Grave has been freed and let go! Oh, I've lost all hope now! Because I believe that the young Duke, to whom I'll remain faithful forever, will now draw the short end of the stick. I'm so upset by all this, I'd just as soon give myself body and soul to all the devils I can call from hell to help me.

The Devil

Ha, ha! I could make some profit out of this state of affairs! This soul is mine if I could just have half an hour with her!

Emmekens moeye

Eest oock niet spijtich

Die duuel

Jaet en[de] grote pijne
Voer den gene die de[n] ionge[n] hertoge hout zijn

Emmekens moeye

Om waer segghen wie sout zijn
Hi en soude ghenoechte in sulcken gheselle maken
Al soude icker eewelijc om in die helle blaken
So sal ick mi seluen die keele af steken wt spijte
So werdic van deler³² ongenoechten quijte

Och adieu orlof ionghelinck ghepresen
Moechdi hier na noch hertoghe wesen
Ic en achts niet dat ic mi dleuen corte
Daer met steeck ic dien opsteker in mijn storte
Met dien horte
Dat ick mi verniele
Paertiscap verdoempt menighe siele³³

Die duuel

Ten helschen ghecriele
In een eewich verseeren
Wil ic die siele onder luycifer broen
Wat dwasen menschen dat si om prince[n] oft heeren
Oft wt partiscap hem seleen³⁴ verdoen
Al onse al onse die iu³⁵ dit opinioen
Hem seluen houden so versteent
Partie en[de] nidicheyt baet der helle[n] menich millioe[n]
Van zielen eert iaer lijt wie dat beweent

¶ Hoe emmeken en[de] moene[n] na antwerpen reisde[n] / daer veel quaets doer he[m]lieden ghebuerde

Emily's Aunt

Isn't it just too aggravating!

The Devil

Certainly, and extremely distressing for all of you who sympathize with the young Duke.

Emily's Aunt

Who's this? To tell the truth, one could have some fun with such a young fellow!
Oh, even if I should burn in hell for it forever, In a rage I'll cut my own throat. Then I'll be rid of all of this misery. Oh adieu, goodbye, glorious young man! May you yet become Duke sometime in the future! I don't care if I shorten my life! And now I'll plunge this dagger into my throat and kill myself!

The Devil

Political fanaticism has damned many a soul. Off to the infernal pack of hell with you! I'll roast this soul in eternal torture under Lucifer himself! What foolish people, who kill themselves for the sake of princes and lords, or because of partisan politics! They are all ours! All ours who stick with one party out of stubbornness. No matter who bemoans it, partisan politics and greed will procure many millions of souls for hell before the year is over.

¶ How Emily and Moenen Traveled to Antwerp, Where Much Evil Occurred Because of Them.

Oen[36] emmeken en[de] moenen sommighe dage[n] / tsherthogen bossche gheweest hadden so reys/den si nae antwerpen daer si corts quamen. Ende / moenen seyde tot emmeken aldus

    Nv zijn wi tantwerpen na v begheeren
    Nv willen wi triumpheren en[de] costelijc teeren
    Gaen wi inden boom om een pintken romenye

          Emmeken

Inden boom segdi

          Moenen

Ia troost daer suldi sien

{C4ʳ}
    Alle die quistgoeykens die hem qualijc regieren
    Alle die vroukens vanden leuen alle die putyeren
    Diet van tienen van vieren
    Stellent int wilde
    Bouen sitten die borghers beneden die ghilde
    Diet lieuer nemen dan gheuen souden

          Emmeken

    Daer verhuech ic mi inne als ick sulc leuen scouwe
    Gheen dinck en es mi bequamere

          Moenen

    Wi moeten daer noch drincke[n] op die gulde[n] camere
    Eer dat wi scheyden en ghijt begheert
    Sit neder troost ia en eerst heer weert
    Twer iammer versuerdet binnen den vate

          Die cnape

Wat wijn belieft v goet man

After Emily and Moenen had spent several days in the city of 's-Hertogenbosch, they traveled to Antwerp, where they arrived after a short time. And Moenen said to Emily:

Moenen

Now we are in Antwerp, just as you wanted. We'll go on a spending spree and live in splendor. Let's go to the Inn of the Golden Tree for a pint of sweet Greek wine.

Emily

To the Inn of the Golden Tree, did you say?

Moenen

Yes, darling! There you'll see all those reckless wasters who go wild; all the ladies of pleasure; all the pimps who live happily by gambling all day long. Above sit the burghers, below the guilds, and all of them like taking much better than giving.

Emily

I'd love to observe such a life! Nothing could be more entertaining.

Moenen

If you like, we could also have a drink in the Golden Room before we leave. Please, sit down darling! Innkeeper, bring us a glass from a fresh barrel! It would be a pity if it had turned sour in the keg.

Waiter

What kind of wine would you like, my good man?

Moenen

Een pintken garnaten
En[de] een pintken ypocras om mijn wijf
En[de] een pintken romenien die verwermet dlijf
Courage gheeft hi al warmen flou

Die cnape

Dats emmer waer een eerst ou een eerst ou
Vanden besten vanden besten met volle kitten

Een banck gheselle

Siet hein sone wat schoo[n]der wyf compt gind[er] sitte[n]

Dander gheselle

Dats waer en[de] wat leckerder druyt va[n] eene[n] ma[n]ne

Deen gheselle

Willen wier ons bi scicken met onser canne

{C4ᵛ}

En[de] hooren wi dat maer zijn meysen en es
Wi sullense hem nemen

Dander gheselle

Hi moet tauont aent mes
Want tes eenen leeliken loeten
En[de] tvrouken en es niet om versoeten
Die es tauvnt mijn eest maer sijn meysen
Suldier niet toe helpen

Dander gheselle

Biden storten ia ick dat moechdi wel peysen

Moenen

A pint of the sweet white and a pint of spiced wine for my wife. And a pint of the sweet Spanish wine. It gives courage and warms the body, no matter how exhausted one feels.

Waiter

That's certainly true! One fresh glass coming up! There! Another fresh one! There! Nothing but the best! Nothing but the very best in tankards filled to the brim!

A Drinking Buddy

Look, Harry my boy, what a beautiful woman is sitting down over there!

The Second Fellow

You're right! And what a horny-looking stud of a man!

The First Fellow

Let's take our tankards along and sit with them. And if we find out that she's only his floozy, we'll take her away from him!

The Second Fellow

He has such an ugly mug, that I'll stab him to death before the night is over. But the little lady couldn't be sweeter. If she's only his mistress, by tonight she'll be mine. Will you help me?

The First Fellow

Sure! You can count on me! I'll risk my neck

En[de] daer af minen voet biden uwen stellen
God segene v brasser

                Moenen

Comt drincken ghesellen

                Dander gheselle

Neen brasser wi hebben vanden seluen
Maer mogen wi hier bi v sitten

                Moenen

Ja ghi al waert totten eluen
Goet gheselscap en mach mi niet verleeden

                Deen gheselle

Bi oerloue waen sidi onder v beeden

                Moenen

Vanden bossche of wter meyerie

                Emmeken

Moenen lief en waert niet geometrie
Dat ic ons wiste te seggene int clare
Hoe vele dropelen wijns dat in een canne ware

                Moenen

Iaet lief hebdi die conste noch wel onthouden
{C5ʳ}   Die conste leerde ick v ghisteren

for you! I'll back you up! God bless you, old drinking buddy!

Moenen

Come on, fellows, have a drink with us!

The Second Fellow

No, thank you buddy, nothing for us! We're already drinking the same as you! But may we sit with you?

Moenen

Why, certainly! Though it's almost eleven o'clock and near closing time. But good company is always welcome.

The First Fellow

If I may ask, where do the two of you come from?

Moenen

From around 's-Hertogenbosch.

Emily

Moenen, darling, wasn't it with the help of geometry that I was able to calculate exactly how many drops of wine there are in a tankard?

Moenen

Indeed, my love. Do you still remember how to do that? I taught you that only yesterday.

Emmeken

Dats waer entrouwen
Logicam leerde ghi mi oeck daer naer
Die hebbe ic ooc vaste

Een gheselle vraechde moenen

Brasser wat seyt v vrouwe daer
Sousi wel weten te sommeren gheringhe
Hoe veel dropelen wijns in dien pot ghinghe
Van vreemder dinghen en hoordic noyt scrinen[37]

Moenen

Si soude noch al meer wonders bedriuen
Haers ghelijcke en sachdi nie binne[n] uwe[n] leuenc
Die vrije consten can si alle seuene
Astronomie ende geometrica
Aristmetica logica ende gramatica
Musijcke en[de] rethorijcke dalder houtste
Si soude derren staen teghen den alder stoutste
Clerck die in parijs oft in loeuene studeert

Dander gheselle

Goey brasser ic bid v dat ghi haer consenteert
Dat wi van haer wat sien moghen oft hooren

Dander gheselle

Ia doch ic weet een paer winen te voren
En[de] biden rebben wilt v yemant hindere[n] oft v[er]corte[n]
Wi willen ons bloet voer v storten
En[de] ghi yewers aen onghenoechte gheraectet

Moenen

Dat refereynken dat ghi ghisteren maectet

Emily

Indeed, that's true! And after that you also taught me logic. I know that inside out, too!

One of the Fellows asked Moenen

Buddy, what's your wife saying there? It'd be the strangest thing I ever heard! Does she really know how to calculate, just like that, how many drops of wine fit into this tankard?

Moenen

She can perform even greater miracles. You've never met anyone like her in your life. She knows all the seven liberal arts: astronomy and geometry, arithmetic, logic and grammar, music and the oldest one, rhetoric. She dares challenge to debate the bravest scholar who has studied in Paris or Louvain.

The Second Fellow

My good buddy, I beg you, give her permission, so that we can hear or see her do something.

The First Fellow

Come on, yes! But first I'll treat us all to some good wines I know. And, by God's ribs, if anyone should interfere or interrupt you, or if you're subjected to any rude behavior, we'll defend you with our lives.

Moenen

How about that poem you composed yesterday,

{C5ᵛ} doen wi ons noenmael deden te hoochstrate[n]

Segt hem lieden datte

Emmeken

Willes mi doch verlaten
In rethorijcken slacht ic al den slechten scolieren
Al soudic gheerne rethorijcke hantieren
Om die seuen vri consten daer met te vermeerene
Rethorijcke en is met crachte niet te leerene
Tes een conste die van selfs comen moet
Alle dander consten alsme[n] daer neerstich[eit] toe doet
Die zijn te leerene met sien met wisene
Maer rethorijcke es bouen al te prisene
Tes een gaue vanden heylighen gheeste
Al vijndtmen menighe onbekende beeste
Diese versteken tes grote smerte
Voer diese beminnen

Dander gheselle

Ey goey herte
Moet v soe seer zijn ghebeden

Deen gheselle

Segt ons doch yet wi zijn te vreden
Met dat ghi cont ey om gheselscaps wille
Ick sal oeck wat segghen

Emmeken

Nv swijcht dan stille
Na mijn beste sal v een duenken ghedaen zijn
Want rethorijcke wilt ghehoort en[de] verstaen zijn
Dus en laet van couten gheen vermaen zijn

O Rethorijcke / auctentijcke / conste lieflijcke
Ic claghe met wanhaghe die di eerst maecte
Datmen di haet

when we ate lunch in the city of Hoochstraaten? Recite that for these people!

Emily

Please, don't make that request! In rhetoric or poetry I can really only compete with simple beginners. Though I want to practice the art of rhetoric so as to enrich the other seven liberal arts, it cannot be acquired by diligence alone. It's an art which must come by itself. All other arts can be learned by observation and instruction, if only one works at them with devotion. But poetry is the art which must be praised above all the others. It is a gift of the Holy Spirit. It is a great sorrow for all of us who love poetry that there are so many ignorant fools who scorn it.

The Second Fellow

Well, my dear lady, how long do we have to coax you?

The First Fellow

Come on, recite something for us. We'll be satisfied with anything you do! Yes, just to be sociable, I'll recite something, too.

Emily

Then be quiet! I'll recite for you a little poem as best I can. Since poetry needs to be heard and understood, don't make me scold you for interrupting me with chatter.

Rhetorica, victorious Art glorious,
I grieve with scant reprieve for your founders
That you are so hated

{C6ʳ}
Ende versmaet
den sinnen die v beminne[n] vallet seer grieffelijc
Hem tfi / die di als dongheraecte
Gheen gade en slaet
Tfi sulcken daet
Ick puer versmade
Maer al eest scade
Ende leet hem alleene die dit aenhoren
doer donconstighe gaet die conste verloren

Conste maect ionste steltmen in een parabele
Voer fabele houdic dat woert en[de] niet waer
Laet daer een constenaer comen notable
donable / van consten niet wetende een haer
Sal claer ghehoort zijn hier ende ouer al
Welnaer / sal dye constighe van armoede v[er]smore[n]
Vercoren / es die loeftutere allet iaer
Maer emmer al hebbens die selcke thoren
doer donconstighe gaet die conste verloren

Tfy alle botte plompe slechte sinnen
die conste sout stellen in v verstant / want
Reyn conste sal elck met rechte minnen
Conste eerst ghemaect ae[n] elcken cant / want
Conste hout in weelden menich playsant lant
Eere gheschie hem alle[n] die consten orboren
Tfy donconstighe die de const vander hant plant
Te dier causen stel ic den reghel van voren
Doer donconstighe gaet die conste verloren

{C6ᵛ}
Princelijc wil ick tot consten keeren
En[de] nae mijn macht altoos co[n]sten leeren
Want niemant en es metter co[n]sten gheboren
Maer tes alle constenaers een verseeren
Dat donconstige die consten so luttel eeren

Mariken van Nieumeghen / Mary of Nijmegen

And berated.
So unkind it strikes the mind of those, your
Courtiers.
Great shame on ignoramuses who
You reject.
For such neglect
I have but scorn.
Yet we must mourn
In sorrow, learning at our cost
That Art through Ignorance is all but lost.

"Through Art, the warm Heart," a proverb
Holds,
But boldly I say it's a fable - not so.
Let a known artist show himself and at once
Each dunce, who of Art has little to show,
Will blow his own horn both high now and low.
Down goes the poet, into poverty tossed,
Near lost, but the flatterer's chosen the Beau!
But know, there are some sore vexed and
crossed
That Art through Ignorance is all but lost.

Fie on all plodding, low, mean wits
Who'd tell you they serve in Art's own corps.
For all shall love truly who queenly sits,
True Art, who reigns on every shore, for
Art makes each land rich therefore more.
Hail to all whom the Arts have glossed!
Fie on the artless who them sore abhor!
This verse then I'd have you first accost:
Art through Ignorance is all but lost.

In princely wise to the Arts will I go
And study them ever the best way I know,
For no one is born to Art, such our loss,
But to all poets 'tis a lasting woe -
That dunces to Art scant honor show.

¶ Om dit refereyn te horene vergaederde[n] veel lie/den dwelck moe[n]³⁸ siende toonde sijnen aert en[de] stich-/te daer selken roere datter een vanden geselscape / doot ghesteken wert en[de] diet dede den hals af gesla/ghen Aldus woenden emmeken ende moenen / tantwerpen inde[n] guldene[n] boom op die merct daer / daghelix bi zijn toedoen veel moorden ende doot-/slaghen met meer ander quaets gheschiede Waer / in hi hem zeer verblide seggende tot he[m] selue[n] aldus

    Wat wonder con ic bedriuen
    Die helle sals hope ick becliuen
    Wat profijts
    Regneeric hier noch een luttel tijts
    Daer salder noch meer haren mont in schieten
    Twaer quaet dat wi dese herberghe lieten
    Want al dat int wilde leyt sinen tijt
    Tuysschers vechters onghetijdige puytieren
    Coppelersen camercatten of sulken dieren
    Vandien vintmen hier altoos planteyt
    En[de] dats al volcxken daer mijn profijt aen leyt
    Dus moet ick mi hier in dit huys ontdraghen
    Ick wil den weert terstont naen³⁹ vragen
    Wat hi hebben wil van onser beyer cost
    Lig icker thuys soe mach ick na minen lost
    Altoos hier ontrent te mijnen ghere sijn

{D1ʳ}
    Ende alser wat schuylt in die weere sijn
    Om int verwaerde te stellen hier ende daer
    Ick doer noch hondert dootsteken int iaer
    Soe crijcht lucifer tsine int helsche estere
    Als een kijcpisse dies staet mi elck te prijsene
    Ick sal oock verloren schat weten te wisene
    Dies sal mi groote eere ghedaen sijn
    Voort alle die saken die den mensce ouer gegae[n] sij[n]
    Die sal ick oock weten te seggen iuyst
    Mi sal volcx nae loopen meer dan duyst
    Eer een maent doer mijn practijke
    Oock sal ick scats winnen sonder ghelijcke
    Mijn lief emmeke[n] en sal mi maer beminne[n] te bet
    Ent mi die opperste niet en belet
    Ick sal eer een iaer meer dan duysent sielen v[er]lacke[n]
    Maer alst hem belieft so heb ick wt ghebacken

¶ Many people had gathered around to hear this poem. Moenen saw this and, revealing his true nature, caused such an uproar that one of the company was knifed to death for which the murderer was later beheaded. This is the way in which Emily and Moenen lived in Antwerp at the Inn of the Golden Tree in the Market Place. There he caused many murders and killings along with countless other crimes which gave him great joy, saying to himself:

Moenen

What miracles I have been able to perform! I hope that's of some profit to hell! If I could rule here for a little while longer, many more will slide down into the jaws of hell. It would be a sin to leave this inn, since there are always plenty of people here who waste their lives in debauchery: gamblers, brawlers, shameless whores, pimps, concubines and other such low-lifes. And that's just the right crowd to provide me with profit. Well, I better stay here at this inn. I'll go right now and ask the innkeeper what it will cost for the two of us. If I stay here, I'll always have everything going my way. And if the opportunity should present itself to create confusion here and there, I'll knife another hundred to death per year. This is how Lucifer in his infernal pleasure garden receives his due. And everyone in hell will praise me for my accomplishments like some famous quack faith healer. I also get a lot of respect for discovering lost treasures. And I'll read everyone's horoscope accurately. Within a month's time more than a thousand people will be running after me because of my cleverness. I'll also be able to amass unbelievable wealth. My darling Emily will love me all the more for it. And if the Almighty doesn't interfere, before a year has gone by, I'll have ensnared more than a thousand souls. But if God should object, then I'll have bungled it again.

¶ Hoe emmeke[n] haer so[n]dich leue[n] ee[n] luttel beclaecht

EMmeke[n] aldus tantwerpen wonende ende / merkende dat si een seer quaet sondich leuen / leyde want om haren wille bi toedoen va[n] moene[n] / wonderlijke veel quaets daghelicx gheschiede sei/de tot haer seluen aldus

    O memorie verstandenisse waerdi dinckende
    Op dleuen daer ick mi nv in ontdraghe
    Het soude v duncken sondich ende stinckende
    Ghi laet die claerheyt der hemelen blinckende
    Ende gaet den wech der hellen vol meshage
    Ick sie ende mercke meest alle daghe
    Es hier yemant om mi ghequetst of doot

{D1ᵛ}   Di

    Ende ick weet wel desen moenen dat es de plaghe
    En es vanden besten niet dit es den noot
    Ic gheuoelt wel al en seyt hijs niet al bloot
    dat een viant moet wesen of niet veel betere
    O moeye moeye v fel verwiten groot
    Sal mi maken een verdoemt sletere
    Eewelijc wter gracie[n] vanden hoochsten wetere
    Ey lasen al eest voor mi wat claghelijcx
    Ick ben te verre al woudick mi te keeren pooghen
    Ic plach ooc maria te dienen daghelijcx
    Met bedinghen oft anders iet behagelijcx
    Ende die deuocie es oec al veruloghen
    En[de] oec en wilse mi niet ghedoghen
    En[de] dat ic mi seghenen soude en gedoecht hi ooc n[iet]
    daer bi soumen oec gheuoelen moghen
    dat hi quaet es om dat hi tseghenen vliet
    Wat wil ic ooc achterdencken besiet doch siet
    Tes nv te verre comen om achterdincken
    Hola ic hebber ghinder twee bespiet
    die ic ghisteren dach stelde om scincke[n] en[de] drincken
    daer wil ic mijn keelken laten clincken

¶ Na desen esse weder gaen sitten drincke[n] metten / gheselle[n] daer moenen soe wracht als datter weder / een doot bleef En[de] diet dede wert van moene[n] geleit / buyte[n] der stadt daer hi noch een vermoerde bij

How Emily Begins to Reproach Herself for Her Sinful Life.

As Emily was living in this way in Antwerp, she became aware that she enjoyed a very wicked and sinful life. Because of her, and with the complicity of Moenen, incredible evil was committed every day, and she said to herself:

Emily

> Oh conscience, oh reason, if you were to ponder the life I lead, it would seem sinful and corrupt to you. You have forsaken the splendor of heaven and follow the wretched road to hell. Most every day I see somebody wounded or killed because of me. I know only too well, it's because of Moenen! He is the trouble. He's certainly not the best of men! I feel certain, though he doesn't say so straight out, that he must be a devil or something not much better! That's the misery of it. Oh, Aunt, Aunt! Your evil, shameless, wickedness has turned me into a wretched slut and separated me eternally from the grace of the Almighty. Oh, though I am sorry for what I have done, and even if I should try my best to change, I have gone too far already. I also used to glorify Holy Mary daily with prayers or some other act pleasing to her. But that devotion too has been neglected. Besides, Moenen won't tolerate it. And he won't allow me to bless myself with the sign of the cross. That's why I feel that he is evil, because he flees the sign of the cross. Why do I want to dwell on this? Just look at my life! Look at it! It's gone too far for second thoughts! Hold on! Those two people I see over there! I invited them yesterday for drinks and dinner. Together with them I'll raise my voice in song!

After this she went out again drinking with her companions, at which time Moenen instigated another murder. And then the murderer was led by Moenen out of the city, where Moenen advised him to murder yet a second

ra-/de van moenen die hem wijs ghemaect hadde dat / die ghene die daer vermoort wert veel ghelts had / om dat hien vermoorden soude. Waer om moene[n] / seer verblide seggende

{D2ʳ}
    Hulpe lucifers kaengie ende helscalps[40] cloue
    Hoe ic hier tvolc daghelijcx verdoue
    Men gheeft mi gheloue
    Voor een groot cadet
    Ick weet al te segghen wat die lieden let
    Ende daer omme te bet
    Volchtmen mi naer
    Ic weet raet te gheuen net en[de] claer
    So ic desen vrouwe[n] wijs maec met mine[n] blasene
    Om die mans na hem lieden te doen rasene
    Ic doe hemlieden den mans sulcke[n] brocke[n] gheuen
    Datser gheen achtdaghen naer en leuen
    Ic hebbe dat hier bedreuen
    Meer dan eens
    En[de] daer en verliest lucifer niet aen ic meens
    En[de] dan beghin ic mi ooc tonderwindene
    Om tvolc verborghen schat te doen vindene
    Dat heeft alree ghisteren dlijf ghecost
    Ic wees hem daer eene[n] scat lach quansuys v[er]most
    In eenen peertstal al onder eenen post
    Daer den peertstal al geheele op stont
    Ic seyde hi moeste deluen tot inden gront
    Hi sou daer menich pont
    Vinden van verborghen scatte
    Ter stont ghinc hi deluen datte
    Maer also saen als hi so verre quam
    Dat hi den pilare sijn fondament benam
    Ende sinen stant daer hi op stont
    Den pilaer sanck tot inden gronde
    Ende daer versmoorde mijn oomken ondre

{D2ᵛ}
    Ick sal voort stellen dmeeste wondere
    Comet gheen belet van bouen
    Men sal noch als een god aen mi gheloouen
    So voer ickse met hoopen ten helschen suchte

man, having convinced him that the victim had a lot of money for which he should kill him. Moenen was very happy about this, saying:

Moenen

By Lucifer's buns and ass! How I drive these folks everyday crazier and crazier about me! They believe that I'm such a great gentleman! I know exactly what to say to fool these people, and then they follow me even more willingly. I know exactly how to manipulate these women, how to bamboozle them with my insinuations so that all the men go crazy over them. I make these women work their husbands so hard in bed that they are dead within a week. I've done that more than once here. And I think, Lucifer hasn't been the loser in all of this either. I've also set to work to let people find hidden treasures. That cost a man his life yesterday. I pointed out to him where a treasure was supposed to be rotting away in the ground under a horse stable, right under a beam which supported the whole structure. I told him that he would have to dig deep into the ground and then he would find a huge treasure. He began to dig right away, and as soon as he had gotten so far that he removed the foundation and base on which the beam stood, it collapsed and that stupid oaf was suffocated. I'll perform even more outstanding marvels for you, if there's no interference from God. They'll believe that I am a god, and I'll lead them to hell in droves!

NA dat emmeken ende moene[n] omtrent .vi. ia/ren thantwerpen[41] ghewoent hadde[n] inde[n] gul/den boom daer wtermateu[42] veel quaets doer hem / luden ghebuerde soe wert Emmeken verlangen/de om haeren oom ende haer ander vriendekens / inden lande va[n] ghelre te besoeke[n] moene[n] biddende / dat hi haer consentere[n] ende met haer reysen wilde / Waer op hi seyde aldus

  Emmeken v bede ontsegge ick v nv
  Wildi segdi eens tot uwen vrienden varen

      Emmeken

  Ick soudt v bidden waert v belieuen alsoe

      Moenen

  V bede lief ontseg ick v no

      Emmeken

  Mijn moeye te nyeumeghen mijn oom te venlo
  En sach in ses och in seuen iaren

      Moen[43]

  daer omme ontsegghe ick v die bede no
  Ick beloue v wi sullen tuwen vrienden varen

      Emmeken

  Sien weten niet alle die mi bestaende waren
  Waer ick ben gheuaren
  Niet te meer dan oft ick waer ghesoncke[n] in deerde
  En[de] mijn oom hadde mi in so grooter weerde
  Ic weet wel d[at] hi menige[n] trae[n] om mi gewee[n]t heeft

{D3ʳ}

When Emily and Moenen had lived in Antwerp at the Golden Tree Inn for about six years, where unbelievable evil occurred because of them, Emily longed to visit her uncle and her other friends and family in Gelderland. She begged Moenen to give his permission and to travel with her. To which he answered:

Moenen

Emily, for now I can't allow it. Are you saying you want to visit your friends?

Emily

Yes, that's what I ask, if it would be alright with you.

Moenen

Darling, for now I can't allow it.

Emily

I haven't seen my aunt in Nijmegen or my uncle in Venlo for six, maybe even seven years!

Moenen

Still, I have to refuse you for now. I promise, we'll go and see your friends sometime soon.

Emily

None of my family knows where I've gone. It's as if I had vanished from the face of the earth. And my uncle loved me so much! I'm sure he has cried many tears for me.

Moenen

Des plackaerts bedinghe dat mi verbeent heeft
Dicwils als ic haer die leden waende vercroken
Ick hadse langhe den hals ghebroken
Maer zijn bede totten wiue metten witten
Die doetse mi altoos ontsitten
Ick en cans niet ghenitten
Dat ic eens pas hadde nae mijn gherief

Emmeken

Wat segdi moenen

Moenen

Niet emmeken lief
Ick gheue v oerlof ghelijck dat ghi begheert
V vrienden tsiene en[de] dat v deert
So gaet rekent teghen den weert
Daer wi gheleghen hebben indeu[44] boom
En[de] morghen willen wi naer uwen oom
Oft naer v ander vreinden[45] daer ghi mi leet
Ick ben bereet

Emmeken

Ick gae bescheet halen
Weten watter noch achter staet int briefken
Ende al betalen

Moenen

So doet mijn liefken
Betaelt vri opelijc en siet op een oneffen mite niet
Vri ten wert te mijnen onprofite niet
Dat wi reisen tot haren oom den pape
Mach icken eens op zijn blote betrape
En[de] ick minen wille mach ghebruycken
Ick sal dien pleccaert den hals verstuycken

Moenen

The prayers of that baldheaded troublemaker have frustrated me often enough whenever I wanted to crush every bone in her body. I would have broken her neck long ago; but his prayers to the Virgin Mary let her escape from me over and over again. I simply never had the right opportunity to carry out my plans as I wanted.

Emily

What did you say, Moenen?

Moenen

Nothing, Emily darling! I give you permission to see your friends after all, just as you want, and anything else your little heart desires. Go and settle the bill with the innkeeper at the Golden Tree where we've been staying. And tomorrow we will leave to visit your uncle or your friends, whatever you want. I'm ready.

Emily

I'll go and find out what we owe and pay for everything.

Moenen

Go and do that, my little darling. It's alright to be generous about it and not question a minor difference in the bill.
Surely, I won't lose anything by visiting that uncle of hers, that priest! Just let me catch him with his guard down, then I can do what I want, namely break that troublemaker's neck!

Waer hi wech dmeysen waer mijne sonder foute
Maer dat ic veel scicke oft coute
Tes al niet en mi die opperst warachtich
Gheen volle consent en gheeft eendrachtich
Boue[n] he[m] en be[n] ic niet een haer te v[er]werue[n] machtich

¶ Hoe emmeken en[de] moene[n] na nieumege[n] reysden

Aldus zijn emmeken ende moene[n] na nieumeghen / ghereyst daer si quamen op den ommeganckdach / des Emmeken seer blide was ende moenen seide / tot haer aldus

        Nv emmeken naer v bede aen mi versocht
        So zijn wi emmer hier gherocht
        Te nieumeghen oec eester heden ommegancdach
        Ghi segt dat v moeye hier te wonen plach
        Wildise niet gaen besien

                Emmekeu[46]

Ick mach gaen tot daer
Maer als om te begeeren aen haer
Herberghe of eenich eten of drincken
Dat en sal ic niet dincken
Si mochte mi schincken
Scandelike woorden wreet onbetamelijck
Also si eens dede ontscamelijc
Haer onwetende woorden onuerstandelijck
Brochten mi eerst int dleuen scandelijck
Daer ic mi nv in ondraghe eylaes

                Moenen

Ick soude ghelouen mijn lief mijn solaes
Als daer te gane dats v ghenen noo tes[47]

{D4ʳ}

Weet dat v moeye wel drie iaer doot es

                Emmeken

Wat dinghe doot

If he were gone, the girl would be mine for
sure! But no matter how much I scheme, no
matter how much I bamboozle her, it's all for
nothing, if the Lord above doesn't give me His
full consent and agreement. Without His help I
can't harm a single hair on her head.

¶ How Emily and Moenen Traveled to the City of Nijmegen.

Thus, Emily and Moenen traveled to the city of Nijmegen, where they arrived
on Holy Procession Day. Emily was very happy about this and Moenen said
to her:

Moenen

Well, Emily, we've finally arrived in Nijmegen,
just as you wanted. And today is Procession
Day, too. Didn't you say that your aunt used to
live here? Don't you want to visit her?

Emily

I'd like to see her house. But I wouldn't dream
of asking her for lodgings or something to eat
and drink! She would just dish out a biting,
disgraceful, indecent tongue-lashing, as she did
before, full of spite. Her irresponsible, incomprehensible words first led me into this disgraceful, sinful life, more's the pity.

Moenen

I don't think that you need to go there, my
darling, my delight. Didn't you know that your
aunt has been dead for almost three years?

Emily

Dead? What do you mean, dead?

Moenen

Ia liefste greyn

Emmeken

Hoe weeti dat moenen

Moenen

Ick weet serteyn

Emmeken

Dats mi groot hindere

Moenen

Tes nochtans so

Emmeken

Ontbeit wat sie ic ghindere
Laet ons dat vernemen eer wi van hier scheen
Siet siet daer vergadert veel volcx ouer een
Scuylter wat wilt yemant vraghen snel

Moenen

Neen troost me[n] salder gaen spelen een waghe[n]spel

Emmeken

Dats alle iaer op desen dach te doene
Als icker om peyse tes tspel van masscheroene
Die weerdicheit va[n] die[n] spele en es niet te sommen
Mijn oom pleecher om hier te comen
Ke moenen laet ons gaen hooren

Moenen

Yes, my darling.

Emily

How do you know that, Moenen?

Moenen

I know it for certain.

Emily

I'm truly sorry about that.

Moenen

Nevertheless, it's true!

Emily

Wait! What's going on over there? Let's find out before we go! Look, look, a lot of people are gathering over there! Is something going to happen over there? Ask someone, quickly!

Moenen

No, darling. They're just going to perform a wagon play.

Emily

Oh, yes! They perform it every year on this day. If I remember correctly it's a play called "Maskeroon". The excellence of this play is impossible to exaggerate. My uncle used to come and see it. Come on, Moenen, let's go and listen!

Mariken van Nieumeghen / Mary of Nijmegen

Moenen

Tes een soete snabbelinghe
Lust v te hoorene sulcken brabbelinghe
Ke ga wi biden roost ende biden wiue[48]

Emmeken

Ey moenen het pleech so goet sine
Ic heb mijnen oom hooreu[49] segge[n] op ander saisone[n]
Dat dit spel beter is dan sommige sermoenen
Daer zijn goede exempelen somtijts in elcke[50] spele[n]
Dus troost en liettijs v niet veruelen
Ick sout wel willen sien

Moenen

Ic en consenteers niet gheerne
Ic heb al vreese bi lucifers achterqueerne
Oft si int spel iet hoorde van deghe
Daer si berou oft achterdencken bi ghecreghe
Bi lucifer so waer mijn hoghe vermet niet

Emmeken

Ey moenen laet mi hooren

Moenen

Nv wel maer en let niet
Langher dan ic v en roepe oft ic vererre

¶ Emmeken quelde moene[n] so langhe om dit spel / te hooren dat hijt haer te lesten consenteerde maer / hi deet seer node ghelijck ghi ghehoort hebt Ende / dat spel begonst aldus

Masscheroen

Bre hierioh[51] masscheroen aduocaet van luciferre
Wil gaen appelleren mijn ghedinghe

Moenen

It's nothing but nonsense! Do you really want to listen to such drivel? Come on, let's go get some food and wine!

Emily

Oh, Moenen, but it used to be so good! I remember my uncle saying that this play is better than some sermons. Sometimes good lessons can be learned from such plays. Please, darling, if it isn't asking too much of you, I would really like to see it.

Moenen

I don't want to allow it! By Lucifer's asshole, I'm afraid she'd hear something which could make her regret or repent everything she's done. By Lucifer, then all my cunning schemes would come to nothing!

Emily

Oh, Moenen, let me listen to it!

Moenen

Well, all right! But don't stay too long. Come right away when I call you or I'll get angry!

¶ Emily, who wanted to hear this play very much, pestered Moenen until he finally gave her his permission; but he did it very reluctantly, as you heard. And this is how the play began.

Maskeroon

Ahem! Hello! I, Maskeroon, Lucifer's advocate, will go and appeal my case

Teghen den oppersten iuge gheringhe
Waer om dat hi dme[n]schelijke geslachte misdadich
Meer ontfermt en[de] es ghenadich
Dan ons arme gheesten eewich versmaet
Al hadde een mensche alle die mesdaet

{D5ʳ}

Alleen ghedaen die men in die werelt doet
Heeft hi eens hertelijck berou goet
Met goeder meyninghen hi comter ghenaden
ende wi arme gheesten die noyt niet en mesdaden
dan met eenen ghepeyse cort
Sijn daer omme inden afgront ghehort
Sonder hope in eewighe pijne stner[52]
Ick mascheroen lusifers procuruer
Vraech v noch eens god der ontfermherticheyt
Waer om dat ons meer ghenade es ontseyt
dan de[n] me[n]sche die dagelicx sondicht onsprekelijck

God

Mijn ontfermhertich[eit] en es niemant gebrekelijc
die berou heeft eer dat leuen is gheynt
die in tijts met berouwe bekint
dat ic een god ben o[n]tfermhertich en[de] rechtueerdich
Maer die so v[er]stee[n]t bliue[n] in erscheden onweerdich
dat si nemmermeer en hebben achterdincken
die moeten met luycifer inde[n] afgront sincken
daer niet en is dan herde wringhen

Masscheroen

V gherechticheyt faelt in veel dinghen
Al heetmen v rechtueerdich god in allen siden
In abrahams in moyses in dauids tijden
doen mochtmen v rechtueerdich naemen
doen sachmen v den me[n]sche[n] blame en[de] beschamen
ende puneren om een onreyn ghedachte
Nv al waert dattet kint die moeder vercrachte
Oft dattet den vader torte oft smeete
Oft dat deen broeder dander verweete

{D5ᵛ}

before the Highest Judge, and ask Him to explain why He is more compassionate and merciful toward sinful mankind than toward us poor spirits, who are outcasts forever. Even if one human being, all alone, committed all the sins in the world, once he feels true, heartfelt remorse in all sincerity, he is received back into Your grace; but we poor spirits, who never sinned except in that one short rebellious thought, are locked away for it in the abyss of hell, without hope, in cruel, eternal suffering. I, Maskeroon, Lucifer's representative, ask You once again, God of Compassion, why we rather than mankind are denied mercy even though mankind commits unspeakable sins every day.

God {The Son}

No one is denied my compassion who feels contrition before his life ends, who acknowledges remorsefully that I am the God of compassion and righteousness. But those who obstinately cling to despicable wickedness and never feel remorse must sink with Lucifer into the abyss of hell, where there is nothing but terrible torment.

Maskeroon

Your justice is in many ways inadequate. Although the whole world calls You the righteous God, it was only in the time of Abraham, Moses, and David that You could be called truly righteous! Then people could watch You rebuke and chastise Man, watch You punish him for even one impure thought. But nowadays, even if a child raped its own mother, or kicked and beat its own father, or one brother accused the other of having committed all the evil ever

Alle quaet dat ye was ghebrouwen
Heeft hi eens hertelijc berouwen
Ter stont es uwe ontfermherticheit verworuen

God

Waer om ben ic die doot ghestoruen
Soo schandelijck so smadelijc aen tscrucen hout
Dat[53] om dat elc mensche ionc en[de] oudt
Ter ghenaden soude staen van mijnen vadre

Masscheroen

Dies hoordi te wesen te stranger en[de] te quadre
Dan te voren aengesien dat ghi naect hebt
Sulcken scandelijcke[n] doot ghesmaect hebt
Om dat ghi die mensche daer met sout reenen
En[de] meer dan te voren dat si versteenen
In onbetamelike sonden horribile
Te becondighen of te verhalen waer i possibele[54]
Die redelike hem int ouerdincken vereysen
Datmen in doude wet niet en dorste peysen
Dat derren die me[n]schen nv wel stoutelijken doen

God

Daer en leihdiniet masscheroen
Het volck es nv in quaetdoen so verhert
Eest datter gheen beteringhe af en wert
Ick sal mijn stranghe sweert van iusticien
Moeten doen sniden met punicien
Ende mijn plaghen sende[n] quaet om verdraghen

Ons lieue vrouwe

O kint wijsdi den menschen plaghen
Dat moet mi wanhaghe[n] mach v verbeden wesen
Laet den me[n]schen doch noch wat met vrede[n] wesen

perpetrated in the world, once that person feels true remorse, he has earned Your compassion right then and there.

God

For what other purpose did I die on the wooden cross in such shame and disgrace, except that every human being, young or old, should be able to enter into the grace of My Father?

Maskeroon

In view of the fact that You suffered such an outrageous death, all naked and bare, in order to cleanse mankind of sin, You ought to be even more strict and angry than before. It's indescribable and quite impossible to number how many people stubbornly persist in clinging to a shameful, horrible, sinful way of life. While the righteous tremble in remorseful fear, others dare commit sins which no one would even have considered when the ancient laws were in force.

God

What you are saying is true, Maskeroon. The people are now so callous in their wickedness that, if there is no improvement, I will be forced to let my powerful sword of justice lash out in punishment, sending plagues which will be hard to endure.

Our Dear Lady

Oh child! Are You condemning mankind to suffer plagues? That troubles me deeply. If I may implore You, please leave mankind in peace a little while longer.

Sent hem lieden eerst teekenen oft verbode
Alsoe ghi pleecht in sulcken noode
Eertbeuinghe dobbel sonne[n] oft sterre[n] met steerte[n]
Dat si beuroeden moghen met sulcke gheueerten
Dat ghi ghestoort sijt wtermaten
Si selen dan bi auentueren die sonden laten
Wt vreesen van meer gheplaecht te sijne

God

Neen moeder dats al verloren pijn
Ick heb dicwils soe veel teekenen ghebaert
Daer si af behoorden te sijn veruaert
Pestelencien orloghen dier tijden
Daermen met rechte voer sonde vermiden
Die sonden die mijn godheit verleden
Mer hoe si meer geplaecht sijn hoe si meer wrede[n]
Niet denckende op deewighe doot vol gheweens
Tes al waer voor sorge ick versucht ic ten leste[n] ee[n]s
Dontfermhertige god wert mijns ontfermme[n]de

¶ Emmeke[n] dit spel hore[n]de wert haer sondich leue[n] / bedinckende met bedructer herten in haer seluen / seggende

Here god hoe wert mijn bloet verwermende
Int hooren van desen wagen spele
Ick hoor dier redenen en[de] argumenten soe vele
Dat ick puer achterdincken crighe en[de] berou

Moenen

Wel sullen wi hier bliuen staende ou seg ou
Wat wildi aen dese brabbelinge hooren
Gaen wi doch minne

{D6ᵛ}

Emmeken

Neen tes verloren
Gheroepen ghetrocken of ghesluert

Send the people first some signs or omens, as You usually do in such troubled times! Earthquakes, double suns or comets! Such strange phenomena might make them realize that You are incensed. Perhaps then they will stop sinning out of fear of even more suffering.

God

No, Mother, you are wasting your time! So often in the past I produced signs which should have alarmed them: plagues, wars, famine, terrible times when it would have been advisable to stop sinning, all of which insults my divinity. But the more I torture them, the more obstinate they become, forgetting all about an eternal death filled with tears. It's always: "Why should I worry? If I sigh in remorse at the end of my life, the compassionate God will have mercy on me."

¶ Emily, who had been listening to this play with a heavy heart, began to ponder her sinful life, and said:

Emily

Lord God, how my blood is stirred by my emotions while listening to this wagon play! I hear so many good reasons and arguments that I'm beginning to feel true remorse and repentance.

Moenen

Well, are we going to stand here forever? Hey, I say, hey! Why do you want to listen to this drivel! Let's go, love!

Emily

No! All your shouting, all your pushing and pulling won't do any good!

Also langhe als dit spel duert
En crijchdi mi van hier niet gaen die wille[n]
Tes beter dan een sermoen

Moenen

Hulpe lucifers billen
Dat si hier blijft staende des versuchte ick
Si sal hier achterdencken crighen duchte ick
Doer die prasinghe die si daer staet en hoort
Ick sal noch wat beyden maer comse da[n] n[iet] voort
Ick salse wel met vuysten van hier doen trenten

¶ Ald[us] hadde moene[n] gheerne dat spel belet te hore[n] / Maer si bleeft hoorende oft hy wilde oft en wilde / Dwelck aldus voorts lnyde[55]

¶ Masscheroen /

O beleeder der hemelen ende der elementen
God inder rechtueerdicheyt in die hochste seghe
Soudi lucifer ende die helsche collegie
Gheen consent willen gheuen ende gehinghen
Dat wi die mensche wat castien ghingen
Van haren mesdaden en[de] van haerder quaetheyt
Anders en crijchdijs nemmermeer verlaetheit
Vanden veruaertheit die si plien
V hant van iusticien moetse castien
Suldi nv onder menschen die bekinde wesen

God

Masscheroen het sal moeten int eynde wesen
Dat ic consent sal gheuen tvolck te plaghen
Want met gheenen dinghen en sijn si te versagen

{E1ʳ}

Voer si den slach hebben op den hals

Ons lieue vrouwe

O sone die me[n]schen sullen hem beteren van als
En wilt niet te haeste v punicie toogen

You won't get me away from here until this play is over. Go, if you want to leave! This is better than any sermon!

Moenen

By Lucifers's buns! I'm groaning with pain because she wants to stay here! I believe she'll feel remorse because of this drivel she has been listening to. I'll wait a little bit longer, but if she doesn't come along then, I'll make her go with my fists!

¶ Thus, Moenen would have liked to prevent her from listening to the play, but she stayed on and listened to it, whether he liked it or not, and the play continued as follows:

Maskeroon

Oh, King of heaven and earth, God of righteousness on the highest throne, won't You grant Lucifer and his infernal company Your consent and permission to punish humanity for its sins and wickedness? Otherwise You will never be rid of the atrocities humanity commits. Your hand of justice must punish humanity if You want to be respected by it.

God

Maskeroon, in the end that's the way it will have to be; I give my consent to chastise the people, because nothing else will instill fear in them before they die.

Our Dear Lady

Oh Son, mankind will reform in every way! Don't unleash Your punishment too hastily!

Denckt om die borstkens die ghi hebt ghesoghen
Denckt om dat buixken daer ghi inne gelege[n] hebt
Dinckt om die passie die ghi geleden hebt
Dinckt om alle dbloet dat ghi stortet in ghescille
Waert niet al om smenschen wille
Om dat si thuus vaders genaden souden gerake[n]
Ghi hebt selue ghesproke[n] wat wildi maken
Al hadde een me[n]sche alle die sonden alleene
Ghedaen van alle die werelt ghemeene
Riep hi eens hertelijck op v ontfermen
Hi sonde[56] ontfanghen sijn met openen armen
Dits v woort menich mensche es vroedere

God

Ick sprac ende ten es mi niet leet vrou moedere
En[de] noch seg ic al hadde een me[n]sche alle die sonden
Ghedaen diemen soude co[n]nen gronden
Kent hi mi met berou hi sal vercoren sijn
En[de] lieuer dan een siele soude verloren sijn
Ick soude noch eer alle die pijne dobbel lijden
Die mi die ioden deden in voerleden tijden
O mensche hier om behoordi te dincken

¶ Hoe emmeken dit spel langher hoorde so si haer / sonden meer ouerdenckende wert seggende aldus

Nv eerst beghinnen mi die tranen tontsinckene
Euen ghedichte ouer mijn wanghen claer
Och welcke wroeghen heb ick ontfanghen daer
Int hooren dier woerden o heere der heeren
Waert ooc moghelijc woudic mi bekeeren
Dat ic ter genaden soude comen van v
Noyt en had ic achterdencken dan nv
Waert ooc moghelijck ick duchte neent
Ick hebbe mijn consente te verre verleent
Sonder redene mijn voernemen ghebruycke[n]de

Remember the breasts at which You nursed! Remember the womb which carried You! Remember the martyrdom You suffered! Remember the blood You shed during Your time of sorrow! Wasn't it all for the sake of mankind, so that mankind could be received back into Your Father's grace? You have said so Yourself! What else can You do now? Even if one person alone had committed all the sins of the whole world, once he sincerely appeals to Your compassion, he will be received back with open arms. You have given Your word, and everybody knows it!

God

I did say it and I am not sorry for it, dear Mother. And I will say it again! Even if a person had committed all the sins one could possibly imagine, once he acknowledges them in true repentance, he will be saved. And I would much rather suffer double the pain the Jews inflicted upon me in the past, before one single soul should be lost. Oh, mankind, that is what you ought to remember!

¶ The longer Emily listened to this play, the more she reflected upon her sins, saying:

Emily

Only now, for the first time, do tears begin to pour down my cheeks. Oh, what remorse I felt while listening to those words. Oh Lord of Lords! Is it possible? If I repented I would be received back into Your grace? I never even considered this before! Is it possible? I'm afraid not! For too long I went along willingly, following my own desires without considering the consequences.

Mariken van Nieumeghen / Mary of Nijmegen

Och eerde ontdoet v en[de] zijt mi beluyckende
Want ic en ben niet weerdich dat ic v betrede

Moenen

Hulpe modicack hoe ick blaecooghende werde
Dit meysen crijcht berou den balck al vul
Ga wi yewers int scoonste vander ste
Een kanne wijns meten

Emmeken

Laet mi met vreden
Ende vliet van mi fel viant boos
Weemi dat ic v oyt verkoos
En[de] aenriep v v[er]ghete[n]de die godh[eit] ontfermhertelic
Och och ick crighe sulcken berouwen hertelijc
Dat nvth erte[57] al[58] besluyten och ic beswelte
Mijn cracht faelgeert mi

Moenen

Hulpe lucifers leueren longheren en[de] milte
Nv mach ic wel borlen blaecooghen en[de] huylen
Mijn meeninghe wil hier al vuyleu[59]
Onder die helsche guylen
Wert uv[60] mijn daet van cleender vramen
Rijst in alder duuel namen

{E2ʳ}

Oft ic droech v ghecoust ghescoeyt in cacabo

Emmeken

O heere ontfermt v mijns

Moenen

Iv eest also
Nv hoor ic wel d[at] achterde[n]cke[n] in haer gaet cnaghe[n]
Tot in twerck der wolcken wil icse draghen
Toornen hooghe en[de] worpenle[61] van bouen neder

Oh earth! Open up and swallow me! For I am not worthy to walk upon you!

Moenen

Oh shit! In my rage my eyes spit lightning flashes! This girl is getting a bellyful of repentance!
Let's go somewhere, to the nicest inn here in town, and drink a jug of wine!

Emily

Leave me alone! Get away from me, you evil, vicious fiend! Oh wretched me, that I ever invoked you and chose to stay with you, forgetting God's compassion! Oh, I feel such deep repentance that it will stop my heart! My strength fails me! Oh, I'm fainting!

Moenen

By Lucifer's liver, lungs and spleen! I've good reason to roar, howl and growl, spitting lightning flashes! My plot's about to fail! My exploits won't be of any use at all to the hellish brood.
Get up, by all the devils, or I'll carry you as you are into the hellish cesspool!

Emily

Oh Lord, have mercy on me!

Moenen

Well, is that the way it is? Obviously, remorse is gnawing inside of her! I'll carry her up to the dark clouds, as high as the church towers and from there cast her down!

Coemtse dan te haer seluen weder
So heeftse gheluck die leelycke vrucht
Her her ghi moet mede in die lucht

{Woodcut E}

{E2ʳ}
Ae[62] dese woorden heeft moenen die duuel em-/meken hoogher dan eenich huys ofte kerke / in die locht ghedraghen dat haer oom ende alle die / lyeden saghen dwelck hem alle[n] seer verwonderde / niet wetende wat dat bedieden mochte

¶ Hoe moenen emmeken van bouen neder werp / ende hoese haer oom wert kennende

{Woodcut F}

Ls[63] moene[n] die duuel emmeken boue[n] alle hui/sen hooghe ghedragen hande[64] werp hijse van / bouen neder opter straten haer also meene[n]de den / hals te breke[n] waer af die liede[n] seer verscrickte[n]. En[de] / heer ghijsbrecht haer oom die d[at] selfspel oec hore[n]de /
{E3ʳ}
was verwonderde wat dat bediede nnde[65] wye dat / wesen mochte dye van so hoghe viel segge[n]de ende / vraghende eenen die neuen hem stont aldus

Heeftse den hals niet ontwee so heeftse gheluc vry
Mijn herte crijchter onsprekelijcken druc bi
Dat ic dit liden aen eenich mensche scouwe
Kendise niet wie es die vrouwe

If she survives that she'll really be lucky, the
ugly creature. Come along, come along! Up
into the air with you!

After these words the devil Moenen carried
Emily into the air, higher than any house or
church. Her uncle and all the people saw this,
and they were all greatly astonished, since
they did not know what it meant.

{Woodcut E}

¶ How Moenen Threw Emily Down from Above
and How She Recognized Her Uncle.

When Moenen, the devil, had carried Emily
upwards higher than all the houses, he threw
her down on the street, intending to break her
neck this way. This frightened the people
very much. Her uncle, Master Gisbrecht,
who had been listening to the same play, was
also wondering what it all meant and who the
person was who had fallen from such a great
height. He questioned someone standing next
to him:

{Woodcut F}

Uncle

She's really lucky if she didn't break her neck!
My heart feels unspeakable pain seeing such
suffering in any human being. Do you know
her? Who is this lady?

Een borgher

Ick sout gheerne sien oft icse kende
Maer tvolc staet hier so en dringt ouer ende
Datmer niet en can bi gheraken
Coemt achter mi heer ic sal ons een gat maken
Dwaes es hi die mi int dringhen slom acht
Siet heere tvrouken leet in onmacht
Si leyt al van haer seluen

Die oom

Dat en es gheen wondre
Helpt al dbloet mijns lichae[m]s va[n] boue[n] tot ondre
Vercruypt mi ic soudt wel betoghen
Die tranen schieten mi wten oghen
Mijn anderen[66] versteruen mijn coluer wert bleec
Noyt en gheuoelde ic mi so weeck
Och vrient slaet mijns gade ic bids v seere

Die borgher

Ontbeyt wat let v heere
Ghi verandert al waerdi puer een doot mensche

Die oom

Om steruen dat ic in deser noot wensch
Och antropos coem en doerschiet mi lichte

{E3ᵛ}

Die borghere

Hoe meslaet di v aldus

Die oom

Och het es mijn nichte
Dies ic therte vol leets ghenoch hebbe
Dit esse die ic wel seuen iaer ghesocht hebbe
Ey lasen nv leyt si hier den hals verstuyct

A Citizen

I want to get a look and see if I know her. But there's such a crush of people, pushing in such confusion, you can't get there. Follow me, sir, I'll make room for us! They better think twice if they think I'm no good at pushing! Look, sir, the little lady lies here in a faint! She's lying here totally unconscious!

Uncle

No wonder! Oh God, I swear my blood has drained away! Tears pour from my eyes. My mind has turned numb, my face has turned pale! I've never felt this weak before! Oh my friend, I beg you, please stand by me!

Citizen

Hold on! What's the matter with you, sir? Really, you're as pale as a corpse!

Uncle

Because I want to die in sorrow! Oh, Atropos, Goddess of Death, come quickly and shoot me dead!

Citizen

Why are you carrying on this way?

Uncle

Oh, this is my niece! She's filled my heart with so much suffering! I've been searching for her for almost seven years. Oh God! Now she lies there with a broken neck!

Och eerde ontdoet v en[de] mi beluyct
Ick en wille niet langher ruste ghewinnen

      Die borgher

Weetti wel dat sijt es

      Die oom

En soudicse niet kennen
Oft meendi dat ic mijn sinnen misse

      Moenen

Hulpe melcflessen van corten blisse
Minen steert ic bepisse
Van rechter quaetheden
Nv en weet icker gheenen raet teghen
Dit is haer oom hoe sal ict nv coken
Ick hadde haer langhe den hals ghebroken
Maer die bede van desen pape heylich
Maect mi den wech onueylich
Had icker macht ae[n] ic soude[n] ter sto[n]t ter helle[n] voere[n]

      Die borghere

Siet heere ic siese noch roeren

      Die oom

Verroeren dat waer boete voer vele ghepijns
Tes waer si roert sekere

{E4ʳ}   Emmeken

Ay mi wats mijns
Waer heb ick gheweest of waer ben ic nv
O heere sta ic ooc noch in die gracie van v
Dat ic ter ghenaden soude moghen comen
Ia ick want haddi mi hier niet ghenomen
In uwer bewaernesse alles machtich

Oh earth, open up and swallow me! Never again will I have peace of mind.

Citizen

Are you sure it's her?

Uncle

Why wouldn't I recognize her? Do you think I've lost my mind?

Moenen

Oh, holy shit! I'm so mad that I'm pissing on my own tail! This is her uncle! How am I going to pull this off now? I'd have broken her neck long ago; but the prayers of this saintly priest made that too dangerous a course for me. If I had the power, I'd take him to hell right now!

Citizen

Look, sir, she's still moving!

Uncle

Moving! That would make up for a lot of suffering I've had to endure. It's true! She really is moving!

Emily

Ah! What's happened to me? Where am I? Where was I? Oh Lord, am I still in Your grace so I can beg Your forgiveness? Oh yes! Because, if You, the Almighty, hadn't taken me into Your protection,

Ick ware in deewighe pine onsashtich[67]
Met siele met liue eewich versteken
Wt tsheeren rijcke

    Emmekens oom

Condi noch spreken
Mariken nichte so spreect teghen mi
Die so menich suchten om di
Ghesucht heeft en[de] so menich claghe[n] gheclaecht
En[de] tallen canten so menich vraghen gheuracht
Ende nv vindic v hier onder dit ghedroom
In desen soberen puente

    Emmeken

Och sidi dit heer oom
Och ghehingde god dat ic op dit pas
Ware inden seluen puncte dat ic was
Doen ic v leste sach sonder dese reyse
Och als ic mi seluer ouerpeyse
Ic ducht dat ic eewich verdoempt ben

    Die oom

Nichte ghi sueeft[68]
Te[n] es niemant v[er]loren dan die he[m] v[er]loren gheeft
Hoe soudi so verdoempt sijn dat waer te deerne
Maer hoe coemdi hier dat wistic gheerne

{E4ᵛ}

En ghi waert vlues in die lucht so hooghe
Segghet mi doch bi uwen ghedoghe
Ick en sach noyt mensche so hoghe dat ic weet

    Emmeken

Heer oom het waer mi onghereet
Dat ic v alle mijn aue[n]tuere soude v[er]hale[n] bescedelijc
Ic hebbe mi den viant ee[n]s ouer gegheue[n] geheelijc
En[de] nae dien ontrent seue[n] iaren met he[m] gegaen
Ick en cans v niet al doen vermaen

Mariken van Nieumeghen / Mary of Nijmegen

I would be already in terrifying, everlasting hell, my body and soul eternally cast out of the Lord's Kingdom.

Emily's Uncle

If you can still speak, Mary, my dear Niece, speak to me! Me, who sighed and wept for you so much; who asked so many questions about you everywhere! And now I find you here in this crowd of people in such a wretched state!

Emily

Oh, dear Uncle, is that you? I wish to God that I could be in the same state of grace I was in when I saw you the last time, before this journey. Oh, when I think about my life, I believe I am eternally damned.

Uncle

Niece, you are wrong. No one is lost, except he who believes himself lost. How could you be damned? That would be too dreadful! But how did you get here? That's what I'd like to know! And just now you were so high up in the air! Tell me, please! I've never seen a person so high up. I've never known anything like it!

Emily

Dear Uncle, it would be very difficult to tell you all my adventures in detail. At one point in time I abandoned myself completely to the devil; from then on I traveled with him for about seven years. I can't explain it all to you.

Ick wilt metten cortsten ouerslaen
Binne[n] die[n] seue[n] iare[n] mij[n] regime[n]t
    en[de] ons bedriuen
Men souder wel boecken af scriuen
Gheen quaet en mach tegent mijne clicken
Ten eynde van alle dese vreemde sticken
Quam ic hier int lant o[m] mij[n] vrienden te visiterene
En[de] met dat wi hier doer meenden te passerene
En[de] ter merct quamen so saghic staen spelen daer
Tspel van masscheroen ic hoorder naer
Emmer in die woorden die ic hoorde
Creech ic sulcken achterdincken dats hem stoorde
Hi die bi mi was en[de] droech mi daert volck sach
Hooghe in die locht

        Die oom

Ey lacen owach
Hoe nichte was die viant bi v

        Emmeken

Iay heer oom ende es ontrent seuen iaer nv
Dat ick mi voechde onder sijn ghebot
Ende met hem ghewandelt hebbe

{F1ʳ}
        Die oom

Hulpe almoghende god
Daenhoren doet mi al dlijf vergruwen
Dien gast moeten wi van v stuwen
Soudi ghewinnen gods rijcke hueghelijck

        Moenen

Ey pleckaert dat en es niet mueghelijc
Dat ghi mi van haer sout veruremen
Alst mi past ic salse met huye met haer nemen
En[de] draeghense daermen selde[n] solfer of pec spaert

Mariken van Nieumeghen / Mary of Nijmegen

I'll go over it as briefly as I can — about the seven years, my way of life and what we did. Whole books could be written about it. No evil can compare with what I did. At the end of all these strange events I came back here to visit my friends. We only meant to pass through; but when we came to the market place, I saw them standing there, performing the play of Maskeroon. I listened to it. And while I was listening to those words I felt such remorse that it made him angry! Him, the one who was with me! The one who carried me high up into the air while all the people were watching.

Uncle

Oh no! Oh dear God no! Why, Niece, was that the devil with you?

Emily

Yes, that was him, dear Uncle! It's been almost seven years since I associated with him and submitted to his powers.

Uncle

Oh, Almighty God! Listening to this makes me tremble all over with fear! If you ever want to enter God's heavenly kingdom we'll have to drive this fiend away.

Moenen

Hey, you damned pain in the neck! I won't let you steal her away from me! If I feel like it, I'll take her, hide and hair! And I'll carry her off to where there's plenty of fire and brimstone.

Die oom

Soudi fel gheest

Moenen

Ia ick hoeresoen pleckaert
Si es mine si heeft haer seluen ouer ghegheuen
Den oppersten af ghegaen en[de] mi bi ghebleue[n]
Daer om moetsi ten helschen gloede blaken
En[de] hoeresone soudise mi meinen tongoede make[n]
Ick soude v hals en[de] beenen verpletten

Die oom

Fel gheest dat sal ic v wel beletten
Ick hebbe hier meen ick in minen breuier
Acht oft tien regulen in een papier
Si selen v vlues doen anders wrimpen

Moenen

Och och mijn borstelen risen mijn haren crimpe[n]
Mits dat hi daer leest wat sal ick verkiesen
Bi modicack moete ic dese verliesen
Hoe sal ic doergoyt zijn met gloeyende wappers
Van quaetheyden so bid ic mijn knappers
Wt ooren wt bachuse blasick helsche spercken
Hier aen mi machmen nv mercken
Als ons opset den oppersten here verdriet
So es ons min dan niet
Ick ducht ic van deser sielen sal moeten scheeden

Die oom

Ga wi mariken nichte ic sal v gaen leeden
Hier totten deken een vier doen stoken
Ic dencke wel v leden zijn v al ghebroken
Mits dat hi v so op vuerde en[de] weder liet vallen
Ghi moet seer ghequets zijn

Uncle

You evil spirit! You would, would you?

Moenen

Yes, you crook, you son of a bitch! She's mine! She submitted to me! She renounced the Almighty and stayed with me! She'll have to burn in eternal hell for that! And you, you son of a bitch, if you try to trick me out of her, I'll break your neck and all your bones!

Uncle

You evil fiend! I'll stop you from doing that! I think I have here in my prayer book a piece of paper with eight or ten spells written on it. They'll soon make you pull a sour face!

Moenen

Oh! Oh! My bristles rise, my hackles stand on end because of what he's reading! What shall I do? Oh shit, do I have to loose this one? I'll catch a flogging with red-hot whips! I'm so mad I'm gnashing my teeth! Sparks of hellfire are blowing out of my ears and jaws. This only proves that if our plans displease the Almighty, our schemes amount to less than nothing. I guess I'll have to leave this soul alone.

Uncle

Let's go, Mary, my dear Niece! I'll lead you under this roof here and light a fire. I believe every bone in your body must be broken, because he carried you up so high and let you drop. You must be terribly hurt.

Emmeken

Ick en achs niet medallen
Dit liden heer oom dies gheen verhael
Ick ben willich te liden tien dusent mael
Meer dan pennen souden connen ghescriuen
Mach gods ontfermen aen mi becliuen
Mi en ruect wat ic doe mach ic eens troost
Verweruen ende gracie

Die oom

Blijft in dat propoost
Ick verseker v gods rijcke tuwer kueren
Wi lesent deghelijcx in die scriftueren
Om te verweruen gods glorie puere
Niet voer een heerlijc berou ter lester huere

Na desen es heer ghijsbrecht met zijnd[er] nichte ge/gae[n] tot alle de[n] gheleersten priester va[n]der stat van / Nimmege[n] maer ghee[n] priester hoe hoge gheleert / hoe expert hoe heilich oft hoe deuoet alsi tstuc ver/stonde[n] en dorste[n] he[m] ghee[n]sins onderwinden haer te /
{F2ʳ}
absolueren oft eenige penitencie te setten va[n] hare[n] / sonden die seer anxtelijck ende onmenschelijc wa/ren waer om dat si alle bedruct waren

Hoe heer ghijsbrecht na cole[n] reisde m[et] zij[n]d[er] nichte[n]

{Woodcut G}

Des ander daechs smorghe[n]s wel vroech be-/reede he[m] heer ghijsbrecht alleens oft hi had-/de misse wille[n] celebrere[n] neme[n]de dat weerde gebe/nedide heylich sacrame[n]t in zijn ha[n]t en[de] heeft he[m] also / met Emmeke[n] zijnder nichte[n] op die reise gestelt na / cuele[n]

Emily

I don't care about that at all! My pain is not worth mentioning, dear Uncle. I would gladly suffer ten thousand times worse, more than anyone can ever describe, as long I can continue to enjoy God's compassion. I don't care what I have to do, as long as I can earn some day His grace and salvation.

Uncle

Cling to that resolve! I can assure you of God's Kingdom, if you truly want it. Every day we read in Holy Scripture that in the end there is nothing better than honest repentance for obtaining God's perfect glory.

After this, Master Gisbrecht took his niece to the most learned priests in the city of Nijmegen. But no priest, no matter how learned and experienced, pious and devout he was, dared to take it upon himself to absolve her or to impose penance for her terrible, monstrous sins, once he understood the implications of the case. They were all very distressed about this situation.

How Master Gisbrecht Traveled with His Niece to Cologne.

Early the next day, Master Gisbrecht prepared himself as if he were about to celebrate mass by picking up the revered and blessed Holy Sacrament. Protected in this manner he started with his niece Emily on their journey to Cologne.

{Woodcut G}

En[de] moen⁶⁹ die duuel es he[m] liede[n] van vers ghe/uolcht maer hi en dorste he[m] liede[n] n[iet] bi comen noch / Emmeken eenichsins genaecke[n] doer dye crachte[n] /
{F2ᵛ}
des heilighen sacrame[n]ts Nochtans werp hi som/tijt half eyken en[de] ander boome[n] van bouen na he[m] / lieden om hem beyden den hals te brekene Mer / ons lieue heere en wildes niet ghehinghen wa[n]t si / dachlijcx een ghebeken plach te lesen ter eeren va[n] / onser lieuer vrouwen Aldus hebben si soe langhe / ende veel ghereyst dat si tot cuelen quame[n] daer si / haer tegen den bisschop biechte. Maer si en wiste[n] / haers gheenen raet want die sonde so onmensche/lijck ende groot was dat hi gheen macht en hadde / daer af te absoluerene

¶ Hoe emmeken ende haer oom na Rome reisde[n] / ende hoe Emmeken haer biechte teghe[n] de[n] Paus

{Woodcut H}

{F3ʳ}
Na desen zijn emmeken ende haer oom vande[n] bis-/shop ghescheiden en[de] wt colen ghegaen na Rome / daer si nae veel reysens met grooten arbeide qua-/men En[de] emmeken heeft haer biechte ghesproken / teghen den paus met weenenden ooghen segge[n]de

    O stadthouder van gode
    Ia god op deerde somen ons ghewaecht
    Gheen sondigher dan mi deerde en draecht
    Eewich ghesloten duchtic wtter hemelscher balie

              Die paus

Waer om dat kint

              Emmeken

    Ic ben sduuels amie
    En[de] gheweest hebbe bat dan seuen iaren

The devil Moenen followed them at a distance. But he did not dare to approach closer or to bother Emily in any way because of the protective powers of the Holy Sacrament. Nevertheless, he threw chunks of wood from above at the two in an attempt to break their necks. But our Dear Lord did not permit that to happen because Emily recited daily a little prayer in honor of our Dear Lady. In this way they traveled for a long time until they arrived in Cologne. There she confessed to the Bishop. But he did not know what to do with her, because her sins were so enormous and monstrous that he did not have the power to absolve her.

¶ How Emily and Her Uncle Traveled to Rome, And How Emily Confessed to the Pope.

{Woodcut H}

After this, Emily and her uncle departed from the Bishop of Cologne and traveled to Rome, where they arrived after a long and difficult journey. There Emily confessed tearfully to the Pope, saying:

Emily

Oh Vicar of Christ, as we are taught, God's Deputy on earth, there's no one on earth more sinful than I. I believe I am banished forever from the Kingdom of Heaven.

The Pope

Why is that, my child?

Emily

I was and am the devil's mistress. For more than seven years I kept company with him,

Met hem gewandelt ghegaen gheuaren
Daert ons beliefde zijt dit bedrijf vroet
Met hem ghedaen so man en[de] wijf doet
Maghic mi dan niet wel ontstellen

     Die paus

Wat dinge kint met den viant vander hellen

     Emmeke[n]

Ia vader lofsaem

     Die paus

En[de] wistet ghi wel als hi vi[70] v quam
Dat die viant was

     Emmekn[71]

Och ia ick dat doet mi claghen

     Die paus

Hoe condi ghi v metten viant ontdraghen
Als ghi wist dat hijt was

{F3ᵛ}   Fiij

     Emmeken

Vadre die goede daghen
Tgrote ghelt en[de] tgrote goet
Dat hi mi dede hebben zijt des wel vroet
Dat deet mi doen al doet mi nv vereysen
Ic en conde ghedincken noch ghepeysen
Hi en deet mi hebben te mijnen behoeue
En[de] noch dat alder meeste daer ic mi om bedroeue
En[de] dat mi int herte den meesten toren gheeft
Dats dat so menich mensche dlijf verloren heeft
Ter plaetsen daer wi hebben verkeert

went with him, traveled with him wherever we chose; and, if you can imagine it, I carried on with him as if we were husband and wife. Don't I have good reason to be frightened?

The Pope

What's this, my child! With the devil from hell?

Emily

Yes, Holy Father!

The Pope

Did you know he was the devil when he came to you?

Emily

Yes, I did! And I regret it now.

The Pope

How could you live with the devil, when you knew who he was?

Emily

Father, try to understand. Though it makes me shudder now, it was the wonderful way of life, the money and lavish presents he gave me which made me do it. No matter what I thought or imagined, he gave me whatever I wanted. And then, this saddens me most of all and for this I'm truly sorry, many people lost their lives in the places where we stayed.

Ouer die twe hondert vadre gheteet[72]
Sijnder om mine[n] wille vermoort en[de] dootbleuen
Als voer ende naer

      Die paus

Hulpe godheyt verheuen
Doer sulcke stucken moechdi wel leuen o[n]huegelic

      Emmeken

O vader soect mi raet eest moghelijc
En[de] stelt mi penitencie eer wi verporren
Mi en ruect hoe stranghe si es

      Die paus

Ick en sal nau dorren
So diep taste[n] in di ontfermherticheit ons heeren
Wat soudi biden viant verkeeren
Sulcken sonden en quam mi noyt vore[n] in biechten
En[de] dan noch voort doer dijn bedriechten
So menighen dlijf verliesen
Ic en weet wat penitencie kiesen
Stranghe ghenoech teghe[n] sulcke[n] wercke[n] sondelijc

{F4ʳ}
Bi den viant te sine tes te hondelijc
O godheyt grondelijc vol ghenaden
Wilt mi doch in dit stuc beraden
Ic ben puer beladen in minen sin
O rechter inder rechtueerdicheit sent mi doch in
V inspiracie wt uwer hoochster glorie
Hola mi compt daer in mijn memorie
Mi waer leet waerdi verdoemt
Roept den priester die met v comt
Dan suldi v penitencie hooren

      Emmeken

Waer sidi heer oom

Holy Father, at various times more than two hundred people were killed, murdered on account of me.

The Pope

Almighty God, you have good reason to live in despair for such sins!

Emily

Oh, Holy Father, if you think it is at all possible, find a penance for me before we depart. I don't care how severe it is.

The Pope

I hardly dare dip so deeply into the treasure of our Lord's compassion. How could you have kept company with the devil? Not to mention all the lives which were lost because of your treachery! I have never heard such sins in confession. I don't know what kind of penance to give you which would be severe enough for your sinful acts. To live with the devil is disgusting. Oh, God, full of grace, guide me in this matter! I am truly desperate. Oh, Judge in Your highest glory, in Your righteousness inspire me with Your holy spirit. Wait! I just remembered something! It would distress me very much if you were damned forever. Call the priest who came with you! Then you will hear your penance.

Emily

Where are you, dear Uncle?

Die oom

Ic stae hier voren
Vol drucx vol ancxten tot dat ic weet
Hoe dat vergaen sal

Die paus

Nv hoort naer dbescheet
Mi waer leet en[de] twaer ooc wel om deeren
Dat yemant verloren ware constment ontberen
En[de] god en soudts oock niet gheerne ghehinghen
Siet daer sijn drie yseren ringhen
Den meesten suldi haer sluiten aenden hals
Dander sonder veel ghescals
Sluyt die aen haer armen wel vast ende stranghe
En[de] die ringhen moet si draghen also langhe
Tot datse versleten sijn of datse van selfs af vallen
Dan werden haer sonden vergheuen met dallen
Niet eer en salsi los en[de] quijt sijn

{F4ᵛ}

Die oom

Dat sal duchtic noch eenen langhen tijt zijn
Eer si van selfs sulleu[73] sitten[74] of
Want si sijn so ruide swaer ende grof
In hondert iaren en souden si so vele niet sliten
Als tvierendeel vander dicten

Die paus

Si mach haer so quiten
In hertelike penitencie volstaende
Dat si van selfs wel selen sijn afgaende
Vanden armen en[de] vanden halse
Maer doetser vast aensluyten

Die oom

Wel vadre ick salse
So vast daer aen doen sluiten en[de] so sterck

Uncle

I have been standing here in the vestibule, full of fear and despair until I find out how it will all end.

The Pope

Now listen to my decision. I should be sorry and deeply saddened if anyone were eternally lost if it could somehow be avoided. Also, God would not permit it. Look, here are three iron rings. Just fasten the largest one around her neck. The other two lock securely around her arms. She must wear these rings until they are worn down and fall off by themselves. That will be the sign that all her sins have been forgiven. She won't be free of her sins before that happens.

Uncle

I think it'll be many years before they fall off by themselves. They are terribly heavy and massive! In a hundred years they won't wear down more than a quarter of their thickness.

The Pope

If she perseveres in this penance, she can cleanse herself of her guilt. Then the rings may fall off her arms and neck. But lock them on tightly!

Uncle

Well, Holy Father, I am locking them on so tightly and securely

Dat si ne[m]mermeer en ontgae[n] te[n] waer gods werck
O priester en[de] clerck bouen alle staten
Bi uwer ghenaden willen wi v laten
Ende reysen weder onser straten
Tonsen lande neder
Van daer wi quamen

      Die paus

Die hoochste beuredere
Die wille dijn liden maken so lancx so sochten

      Emmeken

Adieu heilighe vader

      Die paus

Gaet in gods hoeden dochtere
En[de] blijft volstantich in v penitencie
Want hier bouen in die hoochste excelencie

{F5ʳ} Es volstandighe penitencie seer ghepresen
Bouen alle dinghen daer wi af lesen
Mach penitencie veel griefs ghenesen

Aldus heeft Emmeken haer penitencie ontfaen / va[n]den paus En[de] haer oom dede die ringhe[n] ter sto[n]t / so vaste aen haren hals en[de] ae[n] haer erme[n] maecken / datse haer leefdaghe niet af en mochten te[n] ware bi / ghehinghenisse en[de] mirakele van onsen lieue[n] here

Hoe emmeken wt rome reysde En hoe si nonne / wert inder bekeerder sondersen clooster te Tricht

NA dat emmeke[n] die ringhe[n] aen hadde ghelijc / ghi gehoort hebt so es si m[et] hare[n] oom wter / stadt va[n] Rome gegaen die welcke so la[n]ghe reysde[n] / dat si te maestricht quame[n] daer emmeke[n] inder be/keerder sonderssen cloostere no[n]ne wert tot welcke[n] / haer oom behulpich was En[de] na d[at] hise daer in ge/holpen hadde na[m] hi oerlof ae[n] haer ende reysde tot / sine[n] la[n]de daer hi noch .xxiiij iaer leefde na datti zij[n]/der

that they will never come off, unless it is God's will. Oh, Highest Priest and Spiritual Leader of us all, with your permission we'll leave you now and take to the road again and return to the country we came from.

The Pope

May the Almighty ease your suffering more and more as time passes.

Emily

Goodbye, Holy Father!

The Pope

God be with you, my daughter! And remain steadfast in your penance! Steadfast penance is valued very highly in the kingdom of heaven. Of all the things we read in Scripture, there is nothing better than penance to heal all kinds of ills.

This then is how Emily received her penance from the Pope. Her uncle quickly secured the rings so firmly around her neck and arms that they would never come off during her lifetime, except by the will or miraculous intervention of our Dear Lord.

How Emily Departed from Rome And How She Became a Nun in the Convent of Repentant Sinners in Maastricht.

After Emily had the rings put on, as you heard, she departed with her uncle from Rome. They traveled for a long time, until they arrived in the city of Maastricht. There Emily, with the help of her uncle, became a nun in the Convent of Repentant Sinners. After he had helped her to gain admission, he said goodbye to her and went home. After Emily was settled in the convent,

130   Mariken van Nieumeghen / Mary of Nijmegen

nichten int clooster geholpe[n] hadde dye hi alle / iare eens besochte also langhe als hi leefde

Hoe die enghel gods . Emmeke[n]s ringhe[n] afdede / van haren halse en[de] handen

EMmeke[n] in dit voerscreuen clooster wone[n]de / leefde so heylichlijck ende dede so strange[n] pe/nitencie dat haer die ontfermhertige Christus al / haer sonden verghaf sine[n] inghel tot haer seinde[n]de / daer si lach en sliep die welcke haer die ringhen af/dede Waer af emmeken seer blide was segghe[n]de
{F5ᵛ}
{Woodcut I}

    Langhe nachten zijn selden den ghenen lief
    Die druck int herte hebbe[n] oft swaermoedicheit
    Sijn slapen es grote onruste of meerder grief
    Swaer droome[n] verscrickende of sulcke[n] meskief
    Mi ghebuert vele alsulcken onspoedicheyt
    Wie sal mi segghen die rechte beuroedicheyt
    Van minen droome daer ick in heb gheleghen
    Mi dochte ic was genome[n] wter helscer gloedich[eyt]
    Ende van daer bouen inden hemel ghedreghen
    Daer quamen mi vele witter duyuen teghen
    Die sloeghen mijn banden af met hare[n] vlercken
    Ontbeyt wat sie ic o godheyt vol seghen
{F6ʳ}
    Heb ic v hoghe ghenade vercreghen
    Och ia ic mijn bande[n] zijn af somen mach mercken
    Si ligghen hier neuen mi o godlike wercken
    Wat crachtiger scherm schilt sidi tege[n] tvercra[n]cke[n]
    Dies en can men v nemmermeer voldancken
    Te gheenen stonden
    O mensche vol ghebreken en[de] vol sonden
    Hier aen moechdi nemen exempele
    En[de] ter eeren deser weerdicheit sonder gronde[n]
    Den almoghende god eemighen[75] lof vermonden
    Naer v arm macht seer sempele
    Weldaet dient wel ghedaen in gods tempele

he visited her there once a year for as long as he lived; and he lived for another twenty-four years.

How the Angel of God Removed Emily's Rings from Her Neck and Hands.

Emily, living in the convent mentioned above, led such a holy life and performed such severe penance that the compassionate Christ forgave her all her sins. He sent an angel to her while she was sleeping in order to remove the rings. Emily was very glad about this and said:

{Woodcut I}

Long nights are rarely enjoyable for anyone whose heart is heavy with sadness. His sleep is restless and troubled, and even worse, he suffers heavy, frightening dreams and other miseries. I suffer a great deal from such ills. Who can tell me the true meaning of the dream I just had? It seemed to me that I was taken out of the fires of hell and carried up to the heavens above. There I was met by white doves which struck off my bonds with their wings. Wait! What do I see! Oh blessed God! Did I receive Your blessed grace? Oh, yes, yes! My bonds are gone as anyone can see! They are lying here right next to me! Oh, divine act, what wonderful protection You are against damnation. I will never be able to thank You enough for this! Never ever! Oh sinful, weak mankind! You can learn a lesson from all this and sing the praises of the boundless grace of Almighty God, each as best you can, according to your simple talents. Good works deserve to be performed well in the House of the Lord.

IN deser manieren gods vrienden vercoren
So es dit ghebuert hier te voren
So[n]der faute al eest dat den menige[n] luegelijc dinct
En[de] ghi noch te maestricht in stede ghinct
Ten bekeerden sonderssen daer soudi sien
Emmekens graf en[de] bouen dien
Die drie ringhen hanghen bouen haren graue
En[de] onder die ringhe[n] ghescreuen met lettere[n] gaue
Haer regnacie en[de] penitencie die si besuerde
Hoe ende wanneer dit ghebuerde
Doer die teekenen houdic dit te bat voerwaer
Si leefde noch ontrent twee iaer
Na dat haer banden af spronghen was mi geseyt
Altoos penitencie doende en[de] neersticheyt
Om den oppersten coninck te behaghene
Neemt alle danckelick sonder clagene
Dit slecht bewijs ionste deet bestaen
Op dat wi die hemelsce glorie moghe[n] ontfae[n] Ame[n]

{F6ᵛ}

{Woodcut J}

Dearly beloved in God, without a doubt this is what really happened in the past, even if some people deny it. But, if you went to the city of Maastricht, to the Convent of Repentant Sinners, there you would see Emily's grave and the three rings hanging above her grave; and below the rings, carved in beautiful letters, you can read about how and when all of this occurred, about her way of life and the penance she endured. I believe the story all the more because of this evidence. I was told that she lived for another two years after her bonds fell off, always engaged in diligent penance to please the King of Kings. Accept this simple lesson gratefully and without complaint. It was inspired by affection, so that we may receive the glory of heaven.

Amen.

{Woodcut J - Printer's Emblem}

List of Corrections

The following is a list of corrections for the printing mistakes contained in the Willem Vorsterman edition of *Mariken van Nieumeghen*.

1	In	20	alkemie
2	wi	21	in
3	Groet	22	verfroyt
4	adolf	23	sorghen
5	heb	24	steeckt
6	woent	25	wilde
7	slaen	26	lettere
8	ghetoeft	27	lieuer
9	moeye	28	eersten
10	laten	29	ghemuyt
11	onghequelt	30	moeye
12	scandich	31	moeye
13	versoeten	32	deser
14	boel	33	This line belongs more logically to the devil.
15	verleede		
16	'die' repeated	34	seluen
17	scick	35	in
18	aenschouwelijck	36	DOen
19	ghesopen	37	scriuen

38	moenen	59	vuylen
39	gaen	60	nv
40	helscaps	61	worpense
41	tantwerpen	62	NAe
42	utermaten	63	ALs
43	Moenen	64	hadde
44	inden	65	ende
45	vrienden	66	aderen
46	Emmeken	67	onsachtich
47	noot es	68	sneeft
48	wine	69	moenen
49	hooren	70	bi
50	selcke	71	Emmeken
51	unclear, could be representation of throat clearing	72	gheeert
		73	sullen
52	stuer	74	sliten
53	Dan	75	eewighen
54	impossibele		
55	luyde		
56	soude		
57	nv therte		
58	sal		

Prose Translation of Emily's Hymn to Poetry

(cf. pp. 81 & 83)

Oh rhetoric, famous, lovely art, I grieve in sorrow for those who first created you that now you are hated and scorned. This is very painful to those minds who love you. Shame on those ignorant ones, who give you no care. For shame, such a deed I simply despise. But even if it is a loss and a sorrow for all those who listen to this, true art is being lost by the ignorant.

A proverb states: "Art brings forth affection." I maintain that this is a fable, and not true. Let a true artist appear, then the incompetent, who know nothing about the arts, are heard clearly here and everywhere. The artist nearly dies of poverty, and yet the flatterer is always chosen. But there are still those who are angry about it: true art is being lost by the ignorant.

Shame on all stupid, obtuse, simple-minded souls, who try to persuade you that they practice art, because everyone shall justly love true art, art which is queen everywhere, because art makes many a pleasant country blissful. Hail to all who cultivate the arts, shame on the ignorant who reject art. For these reasons I place this verse first: true art is being lost by the ignorant.

Regally I will apply myself to the arts and always study the arts as best I can, because no one is born to the arts; but to all artists it is a sorrow that the ignorant honor the arts so little.

Select Bibliography

Early Dutch Editions

1. A: Vorsterman, Willem. Antwerp, approx. 1514/18 (Location: Munich, Bayerische Staatsbibliothek). Facsimile reproduction with introduction by P. Leendertz Jr. The Hague: Martinus Nijhoff, 1904.

   die waerachtige en[de] / Een seer wonderlijcke historie van Marike[n] van / nieumeghen die meer dan seuen iaren / mette[n] duuel woe[n]de / en[de] verkeerde

2. U: Borculo, Herman van. Utrecht, 1608 (Location: The Hague, Royal Library).

   Een schone / Historie / ende zeer wonder-/lijke ende waerachtige geschiedenissen van / Mariken van Nimmegen / hoe sy meer dan / seven jaren met den Duyvel woon-/de ende verkeerde. / Op een nieu ghecorrigeert, ende met schoone / Figueren verciert. / Tot Vtrecht. / By Herman van Borculo / woonende onder den / Doms Thoorn int vliegende Hart. / M.DC. VIII.

3. S: Stroobant, Pauwels. Antwerp, 1615 (Location: Gent, University Library).

   Een schoone / Historie van Mariken van Nimweghen / een / seer wonderlijcke ende waerachtige geschiedenisse / hoe sy meer dan seven Jaren met de Duyvel / woonde ende verkeerde. / T'Antwerpen. Bij Pauwels Stroobant / inde Cammerstraat / inden witten Hasewint. M.DC.XV.

4. Str: Stroobant, Pauwels. Antwerp, 1615 (Location: Library of the Duke of Arenberg). A sloppy reprint of S, with the same printer's name and year, but in reality a pirated edition.

   Een schoone / Historie van / Mariken. / van Nimweghen / een seer wonderlijcke ende / waerachtige gheschiedenisse hoe sij / meer dan seven jaren met den / Duyvel woonde ende verkeerde / T'Antwerpen / By Pauwels Stroobant / inde / Cammerstraet inden / witten Hasewint / M.DC.XV.

140   Mariken van Nieumeghen / Mary of Nijmegen

5.   D: Doesborch, Jan van. Antwerp, approx. 1518. (Location: S. Marino, California, Henry E. Huntington Library). Ayres, Harry Morgan and Adriaan Jacob Barnouw, eds. *Mary of Nimmegen: A Facsimile Reproduction of the Copy of the English Version in the Huntington Library.* S. Marino: Huntington Library Publications. Cambridge, Mass.: Harvard University Press, 1932.

Here begynneth a lyttell story that was of a / trwethe done in the lande of Gelders of a may/de that was named Mary of Ne[m]megen y was / the dyuels paramoure by the space of .vij. yere longe. Colophon: "Thus endeth this lytell treatyse Jmprynted / at Anwarpe by me John[n] Duisbrowghe dwel/lynge besyde the camer porte."

Raftery, Margaret M., ed. *Mary of Nemmegen.* Leiden: E. J. Brill, 1990.

Modern English Translations

Ayres, Harry Morgan, trans. *A Marvelous History of Mary of Nimmegen, who for more than seven years lived and had ado with the devil.* Introduction by Adriaan J. Barnouw. The Hague: M. Nijhoff, 1924.

Colledge, E., trans. *Mary of Nijmeghen.* Bibliotheca Neerlandica, Mediaeval Netherlands Religious Literature: A Library of Classics of Dutch and Flemish Literature. Leyden: Sythoff; London: Heinemann; New York: London House & Maxwell, 1965.

Bibliographies

Eeghem, W. van. "Proeve van een naar tijdsorde opgemaakte bibliographie over *Mariken van Nieumeghen.*" *Verslagen en Mededeelingen der Kon. Vlaamsche Academie voor Taal- en Letterkunde* (1942): 435-48.

Roemans, R. and G. W. Wolthius. "Analytische bibliographie." In *Mariken van Nieumeghen,* edited by A. L. Verhofstede, 39-75. Antwerp: De Vlijt N. V., 1950.

Modern Editions

Beuken, W. H., ed. *Mariken van Nimmegen: Die waerachtige ende een seer wonderlijcke historie van Mariken van Nieumeghen.* 2d ed. Klassiek

Letterkundig Pantheon, no. 170. Zutphen: B.V. W.J. Thieme & Cie, n. d., and 3d ed., rev. and enl. 1972.

Coigneau, Dirk, ed. *Mariken van Nieumeghen*. Nijhoffs Nederlandse Klassieken. The Hague: Nijhoff, 1982.

Debaene, L., ed. *Marieken van Nieumegen*. Klassieken uit de Nederlandse Letterkunde. Zwolle: W. E. J. Tjeenk Willink, 1958.

Hageland, A. van, ed. *De Wandelende Jood & Lanseloet van Denemarken & Marieke van Nijmegen.* Vlaamse volksboeken. Antwerp: Beckers, 1983.

Kruyskamp, C. H. A., ed. *Mariken van Nieumeghen*. Klassieke Galerij, no. 66, Antwerp: De Nederlandsche Boekhandel, 1954, and 3d, 4th and 5th eds., rev. and enl., 1966, 1970, 1972.

Saalborn, Arnold, ed. *Die waerachtige ende een seer wonderlijcke historie van Mariken van Nieumeghen die meer dan seven jaren metten duvel woende ende verkeerde*. Naarden: in den Toren, 1949.

Maskeroon

Snellart, F. A., ed. "Dit es van Maskeroen." In *Nederlandsche gedichten uit de veertiende eeuw van Jan Boendale, Hein van Aken en anderen, naar het Oxfordsch Handschrift*. Brussels: M. Hayez, 1869, 493-537.

Works about *Mariken van Nieumeghen* in English

Barnouw, A. J. "Mary of Nimmegen." *Germanic Review* 6 (1931): 69-84.

Bruyn, Lucy de. *Woman and the Devil in Sixteenth-Century Literature*. A Bear Book. Tisbury, Wiltshire: Compton Press, 1979.

Dijk, Hans van. "Mariken van Nieumeghen." *Dutch Crossing* 22 (April 1984): 27-37.

Knuth, Carole Brown. "Mariken van Nieumeghen Revisited." *The Fifteenth Century: Acta* 12 (1985): 51-59.

Strietman, Elsa. "The Low Countries." In *The Theatre of Medieval Europe: New Research in Early Drama*, ed. Eckehard Simon, Cambridge: Cambridge University Press, 1991, 225-52.

———. "The Face of Janus: Debatable Issues in *Mariken van Nieumeghen*." In *Medieval Drama on the Continent of Europe*, eds. Clifford Davidson and John H. Stroupe, Kalamazoo, MI: Medieval Institute Publications, 1993, 64-82.

Works about *Mariken van Nieumeghen* Primarily in Dutch

Bax, D. "Heeft Mariken van Nieumeghen werkelijk geleefd?" *De Nieuwe Taalgids* 38 (1944): 116-19.

Berg, B. van den. "De noordnederlandse afkomst van Mariken van Nieumeghen." *De Nieuwe Taalgids* 38 (1944): 114-15.

Beuken, W. H. "Mariken's eerherstel." *Tijdschrift voor Taal en Letteren* 19 (1931): 111-122.

Brachin, Pierre. "En Marge de *Mariken van Nieumeghen*." *Études germaniques* 17 (1962): 313-18.

Bromberg, R. L. J. "De plaats van Moeyes dood in de *Mariken van Nieumeghen*." *De Nieuwe Taalgids* 71 (1978): 39-47.

Duyse, Prudens van. "Mariken van Nimwegen." *Kunst- en Letterblad* 1 (1840): 62-70.

Eligh, P. F. J. M. "Enige opmerkingen bij de marktscene in Mariken van Nieumeghen." *De Nieuwe Taalgids* 72 (1979): 193-99.

Enklaar, D. Th. "Watter noch achter staet int briefken." In *Lezende in Buurmans Hof: Literair-Historische Opstellen*. Zwolle: W. E. J. Tjeenk Willink, 1956, 101-104.

Gier, J. de. "Oude indelingen van einge strofische vormen in de Mariken van Nieumeghen." *Levende Talen* 270 (1970): 536-37.

Janssen, W. A. F. "Studies over Mariken van Nieumeghen." *Leuvense Bijdragen: Bijblad* 56 (1967): 1-99.

Kalff, G. "Het proza in Marieken van Nimweghen." *Tijdschrift voor Nederlandse Taal- en Letterkunde* 39 (1920): 130-34.

Kannemeyer, J. "Tradisie en vernuwing in Mariken van Nieumeghen." In *Skanse teen die tyd: bundel aangebied aan W. E. G. Louw by geleentheid van sy vyf-en-sestigste verjaardag op 31 Mei 1978.* Kaapstad, South Africa: Tafelberg-Uitgewers, 1978, 34-40.

Knuvelder, G. P. M. *Handboek tot de geschiedenis der nederlandse letterkunde* vol. 1, 5th rev. ed. 's-Hertogenbosch: L. C. G. Malmberg, 1970.

Krap, Frans W. *Emmeken, ik ben 'sduuels amie : neerslag van een onderzoek naar het heksenprofiel van rond 1500 en van het speuren naar onderdelen daarvan in het drama Marieke van Nieumeghen.* Tekst en Tijd, No 8. Nijmegen: Alfa, 1983.

Kronenberg, M. E. "Het mirakelspel van Mariken van Nieumeghen en het Engelsche volksboek." *De Nieuwe Taalgids* 23 (1929): 24-43.

Leendertz, Pieter. *Middelnederlandsche dramatische poëzie.* Bibliotheek van middelnederlandsche letterkunde, 2 vols. Leiden: A. W. Sijthoff, 1907.

———. "Mariken van Nieumeghen." *Tijdschrift voor Nederlandse Taal- en Letterkunde* 37 (1918): 241-59.

Mak, J. J. *De Rederijkers.* Patria: Vaderlandsche Cultuurgeschiedenis in Monografieen. Amsterdam: P. N. Van Kampen & Zoon, 1944.

———. "Het process in de hemel als strijdgedicht." In *Retoricale Studien 1946-56.* Zwolle: Uyt Ionsten Versaemt, 1957, 7-27.

———. "Het ringmirakel in Mariken van Nieumeghen." *Levende Talen* 224 (1964): 190-191.

Maximilianus, P. "Over vorm en auteur van Mariken van Nieumeghen." *Tijdschrift voor Nederlandse Taal- en Letterkunde* 68 (1950): 161-79.

Meeuwesse, K. "De bescheidenheidsformule in Mariken van Nieumeghen." *De Nieuwe Taalgids* 49 (1956): 301-02.

Mierlo, J. van. "Anna Bijns en de volksliteratuur in haar jeugd te Antwerpen." *Verslagen en Mededeelingen der Koninklijke Vlaamsche Academie voor Taal- en Letterkunde* (1955): 329-72.

Muller, J. W. "Een en ander over Mariken van Nieumeghen." *Taal en Letteren* 15 (1905): 225-48.

Nijhof, A. "De strofische vormen in de Mariken van Nieumeghen." *Levende Talen* 230 (1965): 368-370.

Peeters, L. "Mariken van Nieumeghen en de Antwerpse volksboekcultuur." *Spiegel der Letteren* 25. 2 (1983): 81-97.

─────. "Mariken van Nieumeghen: Historia - Retorica - Ethica." *Spiegel der Letteren* 26. 3-4 (1984): 179-197.

Pleij, Herman. "Mariken van Nieumeghen en de Doperij." *Spektator: Tijdschrift voor Neerlandistiek* 3 (1973): 232-33.

Roose, L. "Is Anna Bijns ook de auteur van volksboeken, met name van Floris ende Blanceflour en Mariken van Nieumeghen?" Gent: *Jaarboek De Fonteine* (1950) 42-54.

Walch, J. L. "Nog eens: het proza in Mariken van Nieumeghen." *Tijdschrift voor Nederlandse Taal- en Letterkunde* 40 (1921): 220-31.

Wolthuis, G. W. *Duivelskunsten en Sprookjesgestalten: Studien over Literatuur en Folklore: Mariken van Nieumeghen.* Amsterdam: V. H. C. de Boer Jr., 1952.

Worp, J. A. *Geschiedenis van het drama en het toneel in Nederland.* vol. 1. Groningen: J. B. Wolters, 1904.

─────. "Is de Mariken van Nieumeghen geschreven om vertoond te worden?" *Tijdschrift voor Nederlandse Taal- en Letterkunde* 36 (1917): 152-57.